MICROECONOMIC PRINCIPLES
(ECON 102)

Class Handouts and Class Activities
Second Edition

Jose J. Vazquez-Cognet, PhD
Department of Economics
University of Illinois at Urbana-Champaign

Copyright © 2007, 2009 by Jose J. Vazquez-Cognet

ISBN 978-0-7575-6179-5

Kendall/Hunt Publishing Company has the exclusive rights to reproduce this work, to prepare derivative works from this work, to publicly distribute this work, to publicly perform this work and to publicly display this work.

All rights reserved. No part of this publication may be reproduced, stored in a retrieval system, or transmitted, in any form or by any means, electronic, mechanical, photocopying, recording, or otherwise, without the prior written permission of the copyright owner.

Printed in the United States of America
10 9 8 7 6 5 4 3 2 1

CONTENTS

Part I: CLASS HANDOUTS

Demand 3
Supply 11
Market Equilibrium 18
Changes to the Market Equilibrium 20
Consumer Surplus 23
Production 46

PART II CLASS ACTIVITIES

Two Important Economic Principles 61
Our First Model: the Production Possibilities Frontier 65
Why do we trade? To write more essays and socialize more 73
Supply and Demand for Fighting Illini Basketball Tickets 77
Supply and Demand for Fighting Illini Basketball Tickets 83
Should Drug Use Be Legalized? 87
Should Drug Use Be Legalized? (A More Formal Approach) 93
How Uncle Sam Could Ease the Organ Shortage? 99
How Uncle Sam Could Ease the Organ Shortage (Part II)? 101
Who Should Pay for the Gas tax? 105
More about Taxes 109
Managing Your Business Part I: Understanding the Costs of Staying in
    Business 113
Managing Your Business Part II: Choosing How Much to Produce 129
Monopoly 133
Externalities: the Economics of Pollution 139
Externalities: the private Solution (Coase Theorem) 143
The Tragedy of the Commons 147
Public Goods and Common Resources 149

PART I

CLASS HANDOUTS

The Supply and Demand Model

I. DEMAND

The six factors determining the demand for any good are:
1. Price
2. Income
3. Price of related goods
4. Number of Buyers
5. Preferences (or Tastes) of Buyers
6. Buyers' Expectations

1. Price

The law of demand says that the quantity demanded (consumption) for any good[1] decreases as the price increases and vice versa.

The demand schedule is a table with two columns: one for price and another one with the quantity demanded at each price. The following is an example of a demand schedule for good X.

Price of X	Quantity of X Demanded
$50	0
$40	5
$30	10
$20	15
$10	20
0	25

---

[1] From now on, the word "good" should refer to both goods and services.

The demand curve is a graphical representation of the demand schedule. We typically use a diagram with quantity on the horizontal axis (X) and price in the vertical axis (Y). The following is the demand curve for the demand schedule given above

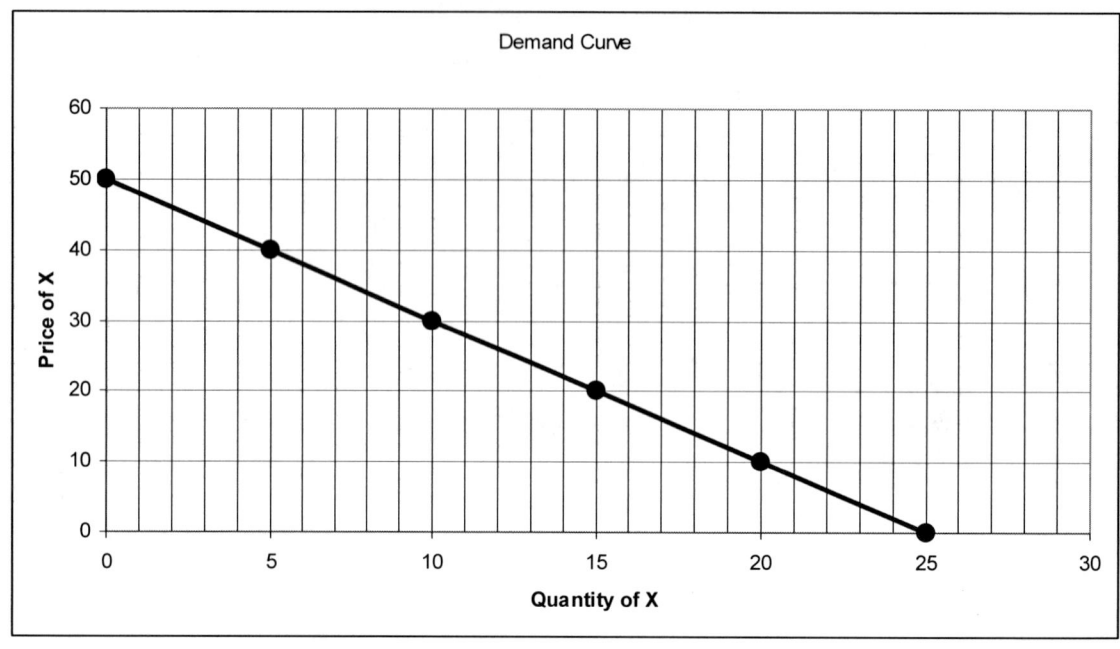

An increase in the price causes a ***decrease in the quantity demanded*** (consumption) and hence a ***movement down*** along the demand curve.

Price of X	Quantity of X Demanded
$50	0
$40	5
$30	**10**
$20	15
$10	20
0	25

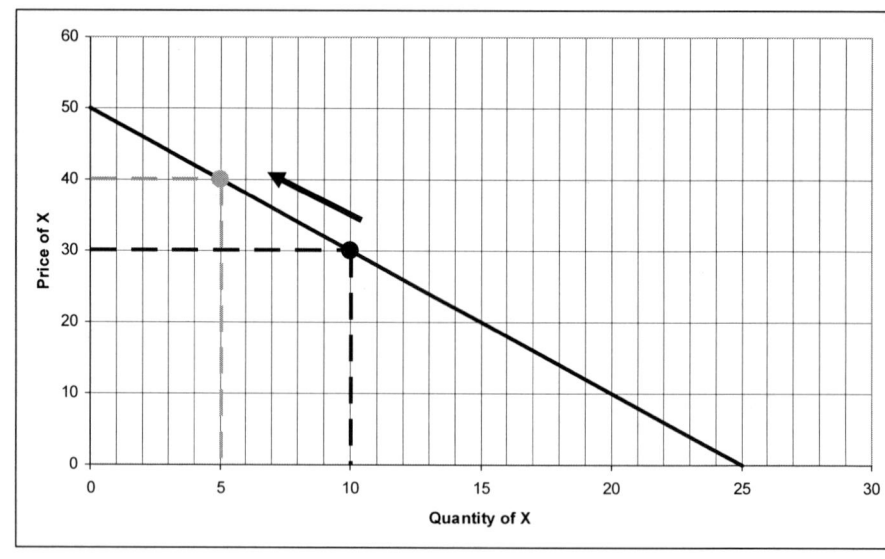

A decrease in the price causes an increase in the quantity demanded (consumption) and hence a movement up along the demand curve.

Price of X	Quantity of X Demanded
$50	0
$40	5
$30	**10**
$20	15
$10	20
0	25

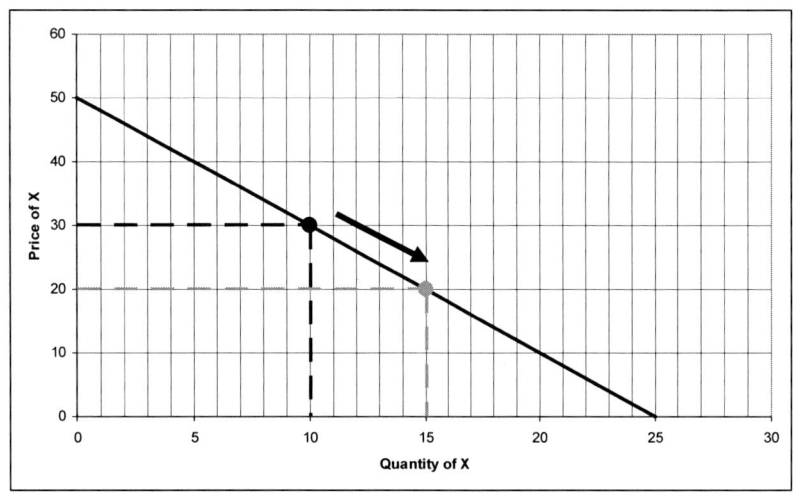

Bottom Line

An change in price = movement along the demand curve

2. Income

An increase in income for a normal good (i.e., apples) increases the quantity demanded at every price and hence shifts the demand curve to the right.

Price of X	Quantity of X Demanded Before Change	Quantity of X Demanded After Change
50	0	5
40	5	10
30	10	15
20	15	20
10	20	25
0	25	30

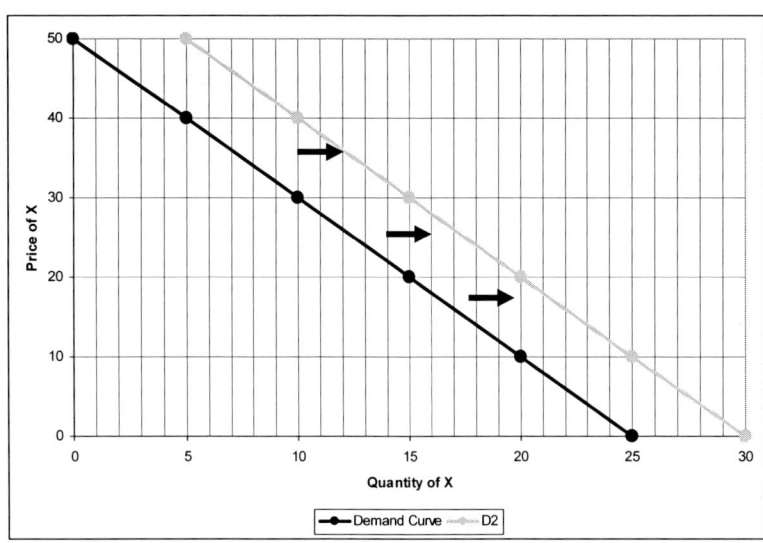

A decrease in income for a normal good (i.e., apples) decreases the quantity demanded at every price and hence shifts the demand curve to the left.

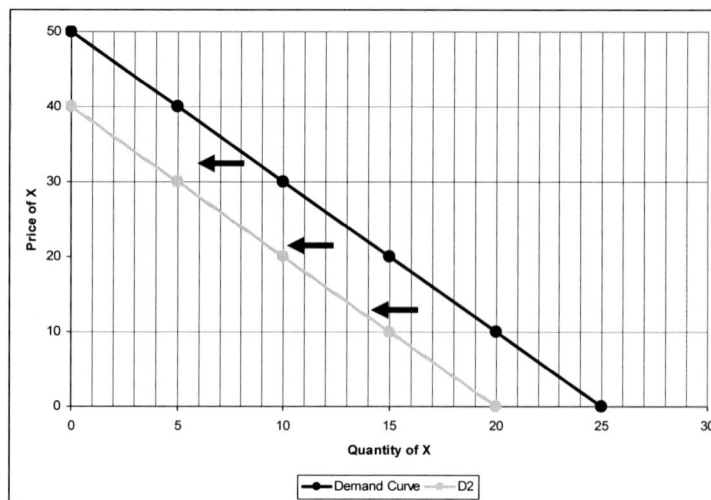

Price of X	Quantity of X Demanded Before Change	Quantity of X Demanded After Change
50	0	0
40	5	0
30	10	5
20	15	10
10	20	15
0	25	20

Changes in income for inferior goods (i.e., public transportation) have the opposite effect of changes in income for normal goods (i.e., increase in income for inferior good shifts demand curve to the left).

Important Terminology to Remember
An increase in the quantity demanded at every price is called: *an increase in demand*.
A decrease in the quantity demanded at every price is called: *a decrease in demand*.

Bottom Line

An change in income = shifts of the demand curve

3. Price of Related Goods

When two goods are *substitutes* (i.e., butter and margarine) an increase in the price of one of the goods increases the demand for the other good, and vice versa.

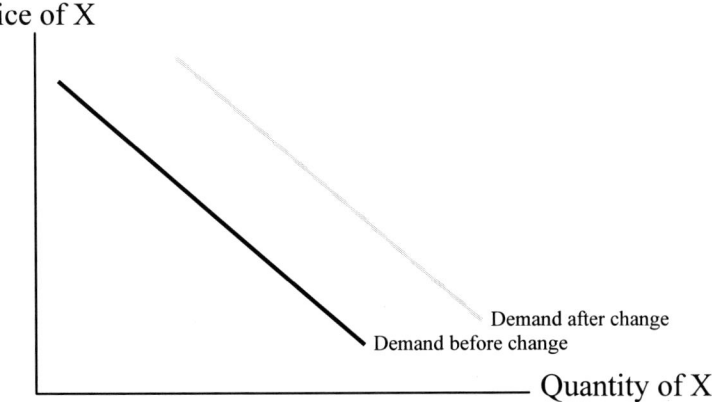

When two goods are *complements* (i.e., peanut butter and jelly) an increase in the price of one of the goods decreases the demand for the other good, and vice versa.

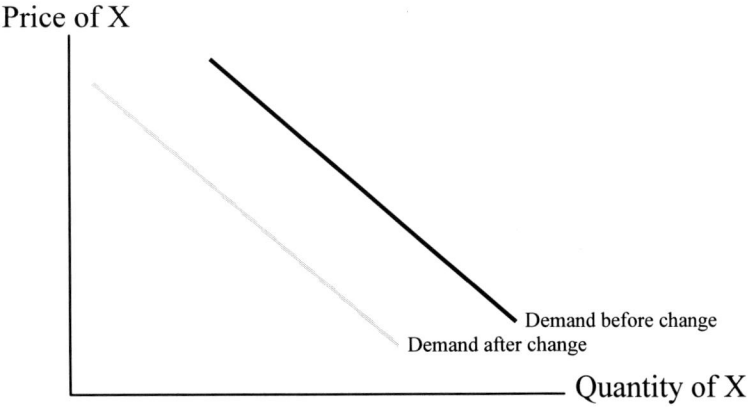

> ### Bottom Line
>
> A change in the price of one of the related goods = shifts of the demand curve for the other good.

4. Number of Buyers

An increase in the number of buyers increases the demand for any good.

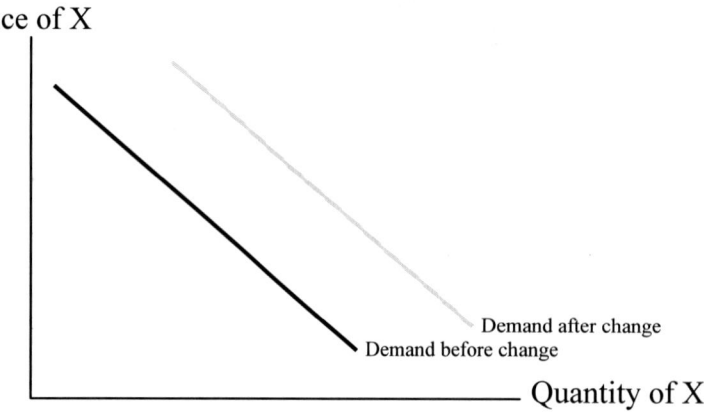

A decrease in the number of buyers decreases the demand for any good.

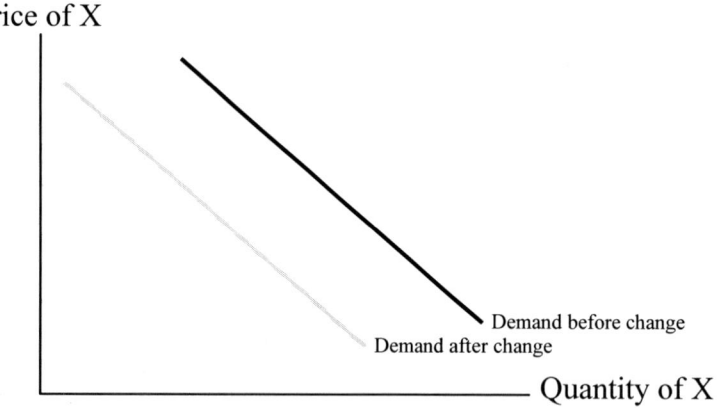

> ### Bottom Line
>
> A change in the number of consumers = shifts of the demand curve.

5. Preferences (or Tastes) of Buyers

An increase in preference buyers have over a good increases the demand for that good.

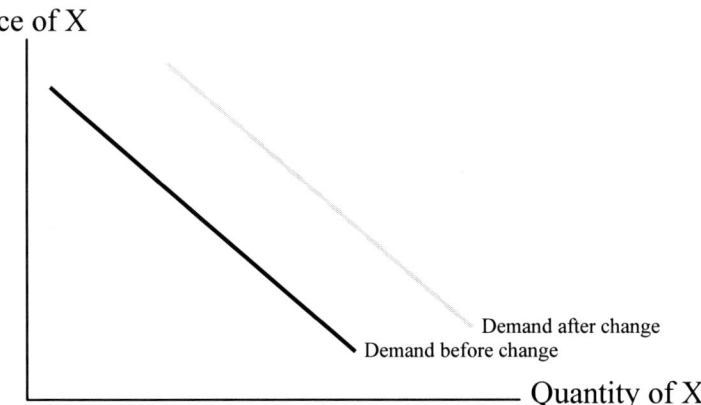

A decrease in the preference buyers have for a good and the demand for that good.

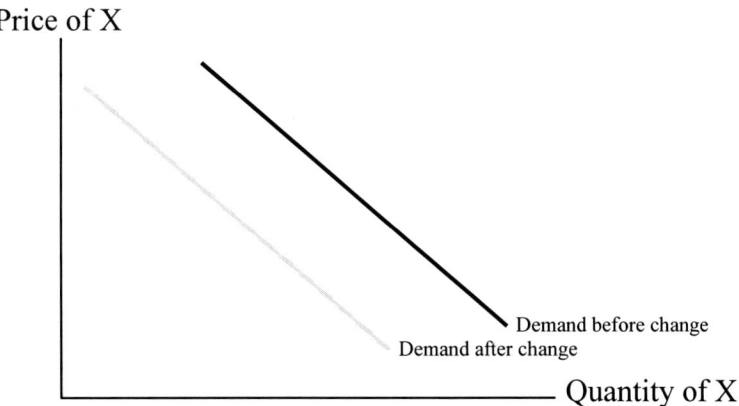

> Bottom Line
>
> A change in the preference of consumers = shifts of the demand curve.

6. Buyers' Expectations

If buyers expect prices for a particular good to be higher in the future the demand for good in the present will increase.

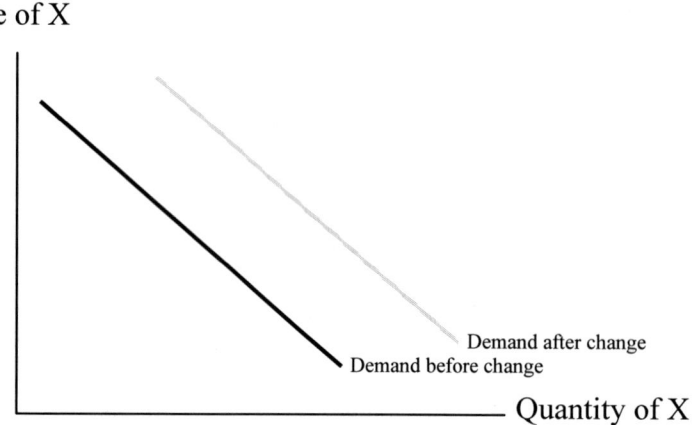

If buyers expect prices for a particular good to be lower in the future the demand for good in the present will decrease.

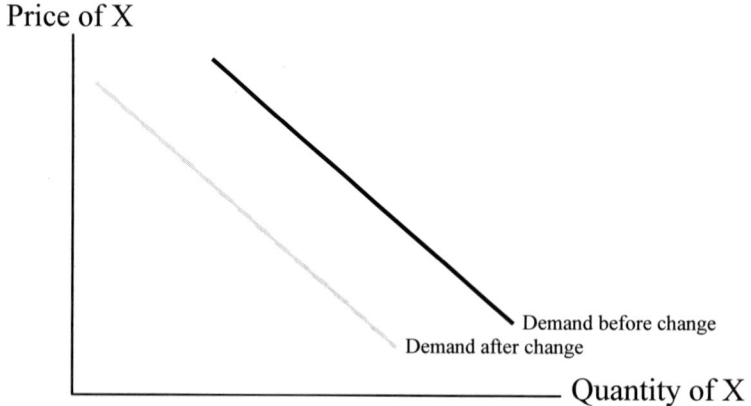

Bottom Line

A change in the expectations consumers have about the price in the future = shifts of the demand curve in the present

II. SUPPLY

The five factors determining the demand for any good are:
1. Price
2. Price of Inputs
3. Technology
4. Number of Sellers
5. Sellers' Expectations

1. <u>Price</u>

The law of supply says that the quantity supplied for any good increases as the price increases and vice versa.

The supply schedule is a table with two columns: one for price and another one with the quantity supplied at each price. The following is an example of a supply schedule for good X.

Price of X	Quantity of X Supplied
$0	0
$10	5
$20	10
$30	15
$40	20
$50	25

The supply curve is a graphical representation of the supply schedule. We typically use a diagram with quantity on the horizontal axis (X) and price in the vertical axis (Y). The following is the supply curve for the supply schedule given above

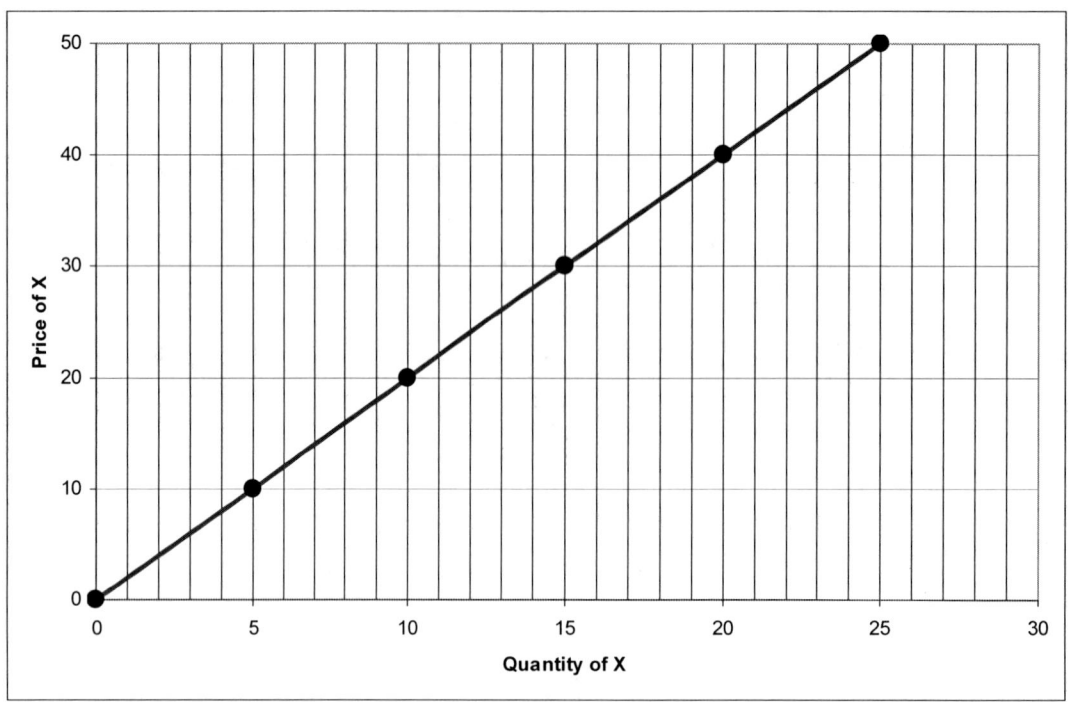

An increase in the price causes an ***increase in the quantity supplied*** and hence a ***movement up*** along the supply curve.

Price of X	Quantity of X Supplied
$0	0
$10	5
$20	**10**
$30	15
$40	20
$50	25

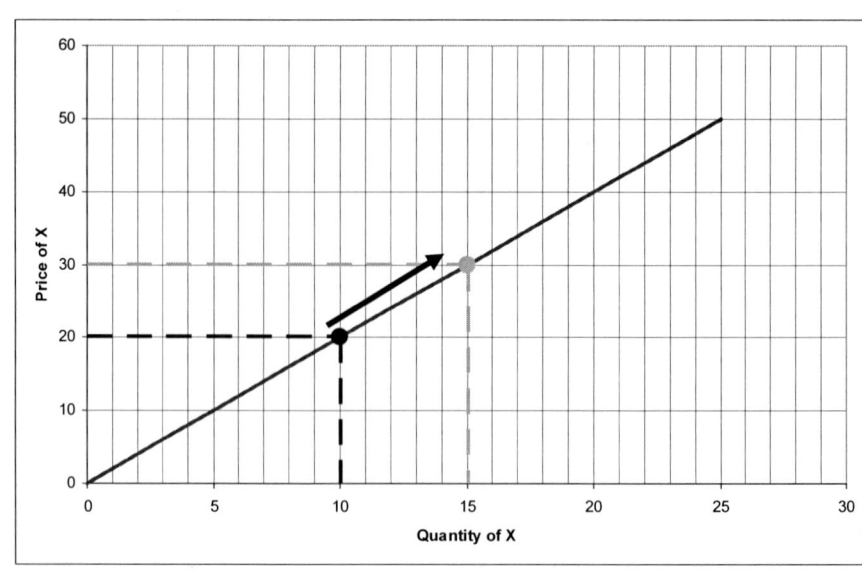

A decrease in the price causes a decrease in the quantity supplied and hence a movement down along the supply curve.

Price of X	Quantity of X Supplied
$0	0
$10	5
$20	**10**
$30	15
$40	20
$50	25

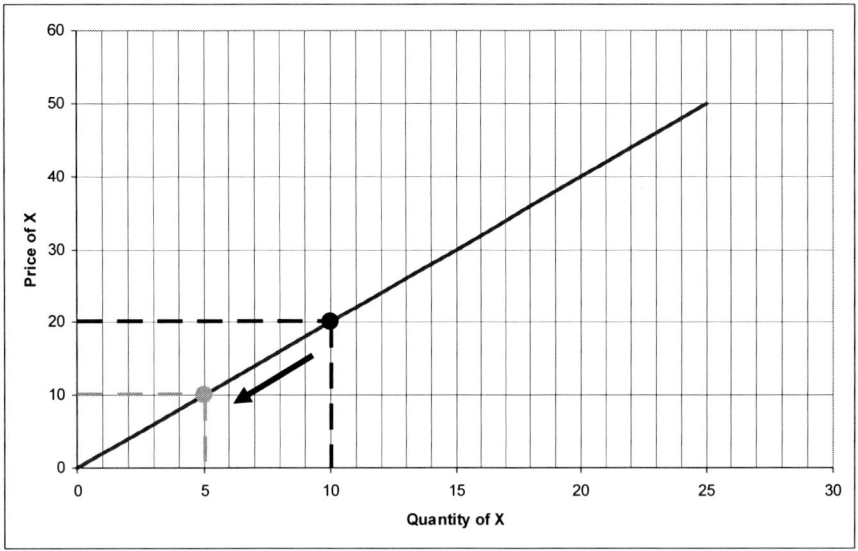

Bottom Line

An change in price = movement along the supply curve

2. Price of Inputs

A decrease in the price of any of the inputs needed to produce a good increases the quantity supplied at every price and hence shifts the supply curve to the right.

Price of X	Quantity of X Supplied Before Change	Quantity of X Supplied After Change
0	0	5
10	5	10
20	10	15
30	15	20
40	20	25
50	25	30

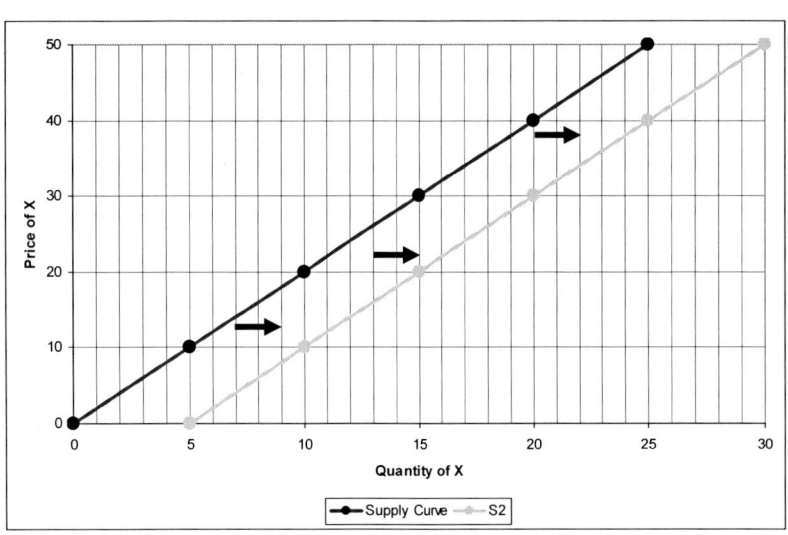

13

An increase in any of the inputs needed to produce a good decreases the quantity supplied at every price and hence shifts the supply curve to the right.

Price of X	Quantity of X Supplied Before Change	Quantity of X Supplied After Change
0	0	0
10	5	0
20	10	5
30	15	10
40	20	15
50	25	20

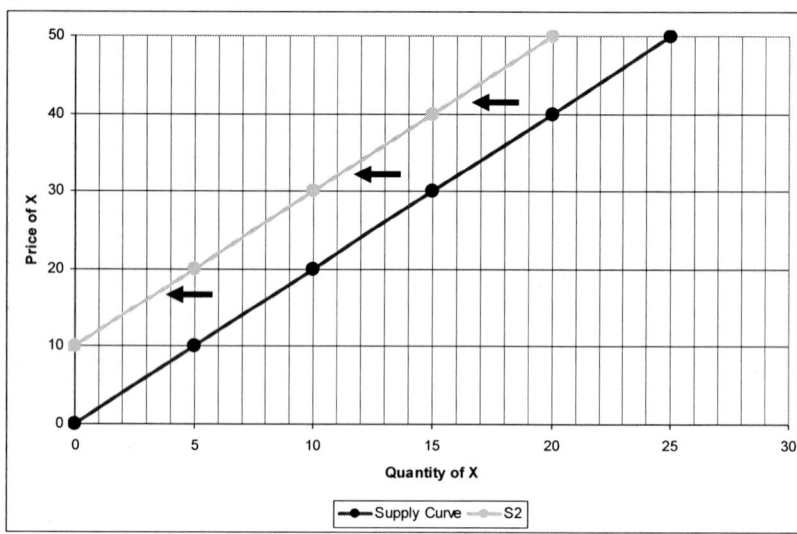

Important Terminology to Remember
An increase in the quantity supplied at every price is called: *an increase in supply.*
A decrease in the quantity supplied at every price is called: *a decrease in supply.*

Bottom Line

An change in price of inputs = shifts of the supply curve

3. Technology

An improvement in the technology use to produce a good increases the supply for that good.

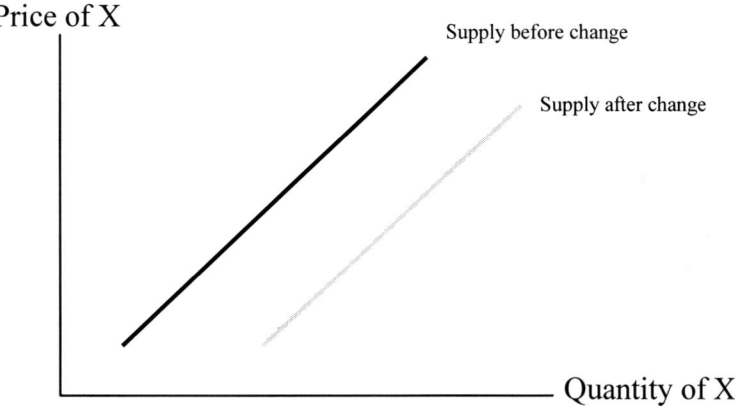

> **Bottom Line**
>
> A change in the technology use to produce a good = shifts of the supply curve for the other good.

4. Number of Sellers

An increase in the number of sellers increases the supply for any good.

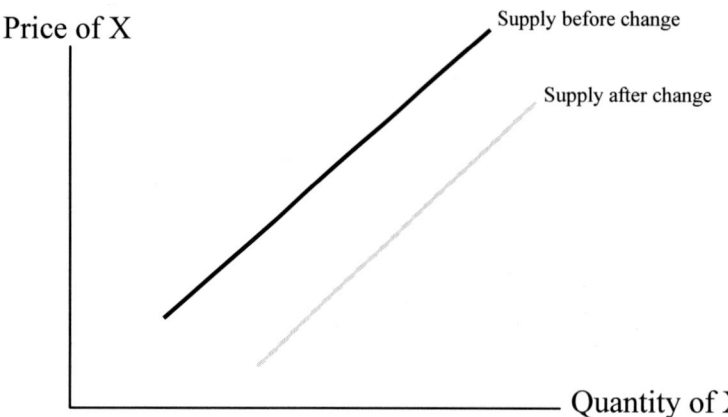

A decrease in the number of sellers decreases the supply for any good.

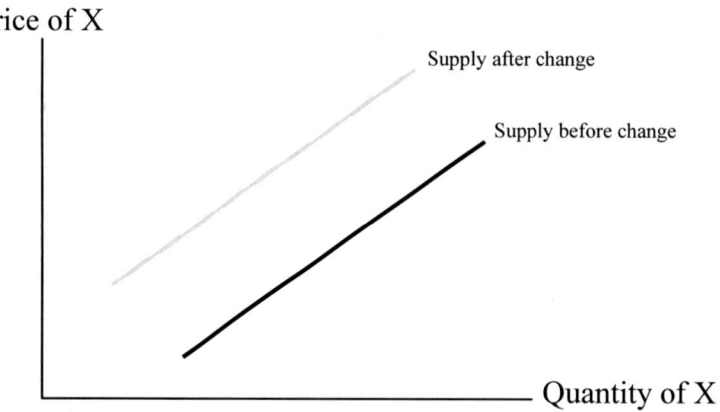

Bottom Line

A change in the number of sellers = shifts of the supply curve.

5. Sellers' Expectations

If sellers expect prices for a particular good to be higher in the future the supply for good in the present will decrease.

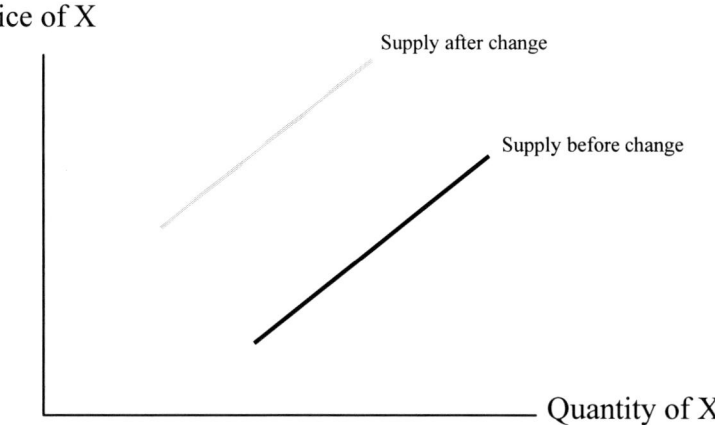

If sellers expect prices for a particular good to be lower in the future the supply for good in the present will increase.

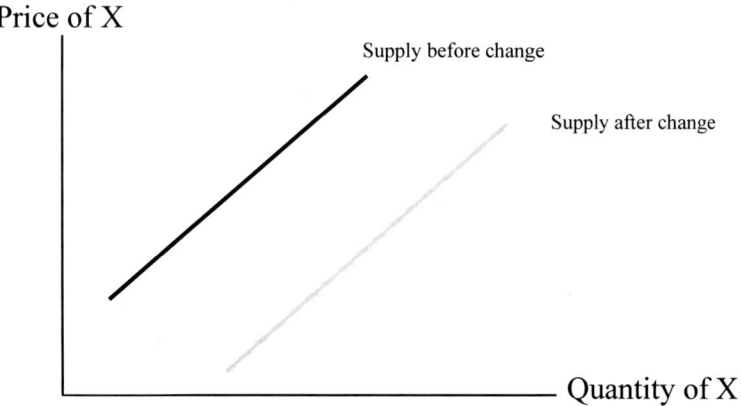

> ### Bottom Line
> A change in the expectations sellers have about the price in the future = shifts of the supply curve in the present

III. MARKET EQUILIBRIUM

The market is in *equilibrium* when the quantity demanded and the quantity supplied are equal.

The quantity in the market at the market equilibrium is called the *equilibrium quantity*.

The quantity in the market at the market equilibrium is called the *equilibrium quantity*.

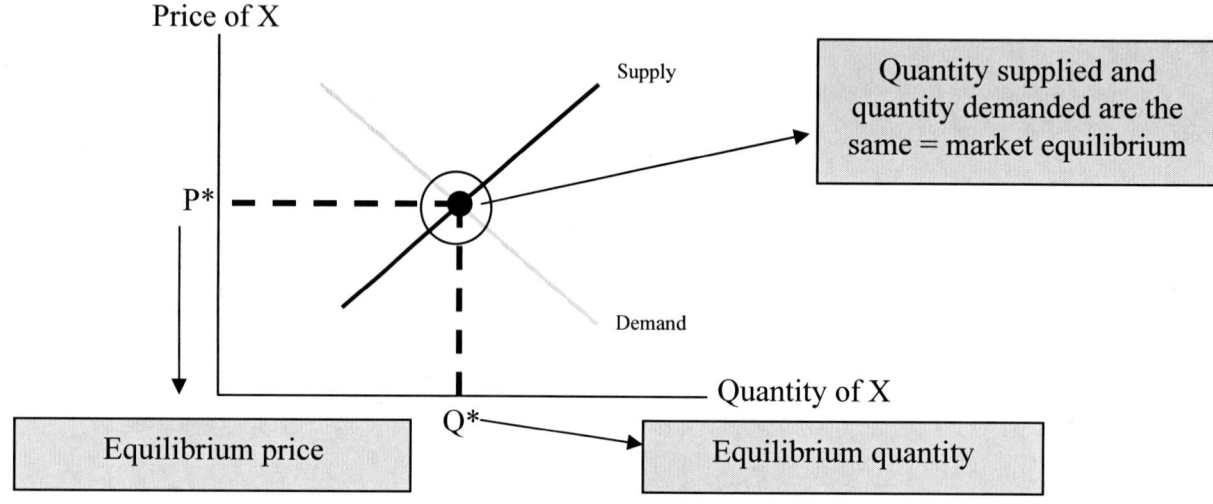

When the actual price is above the equilibrium price we have a **supply surplus**.

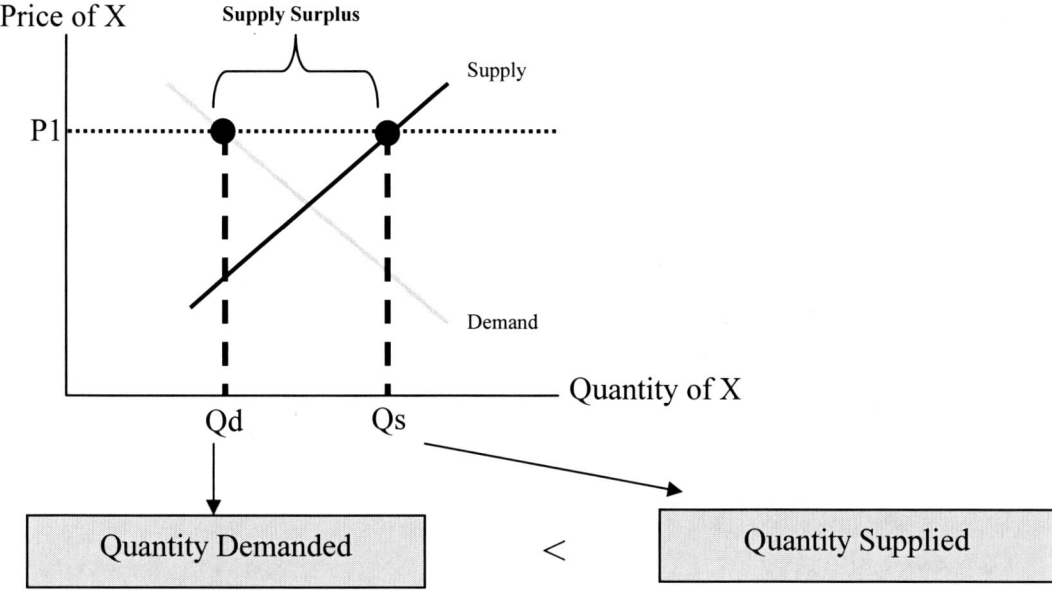

When the actual price is below the equilibrium price we have a **supply shortage**.

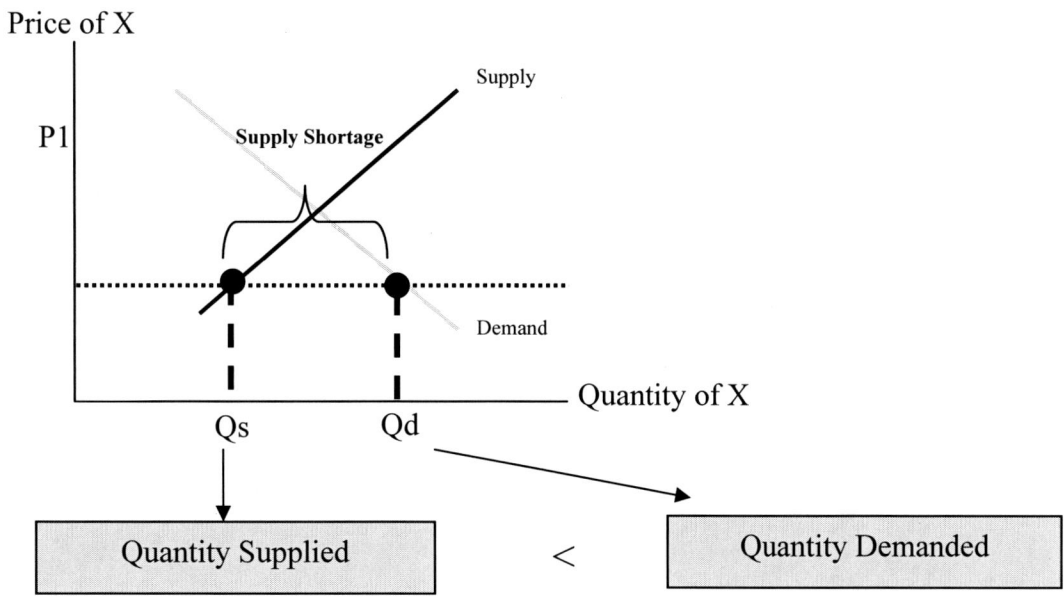

IV. CHANGES TO THE MARKET EQUILIBRIUM

If the market is at equilibrium, an increase in the demand curve will increase the equilibrium quantity and the equilibrium price.

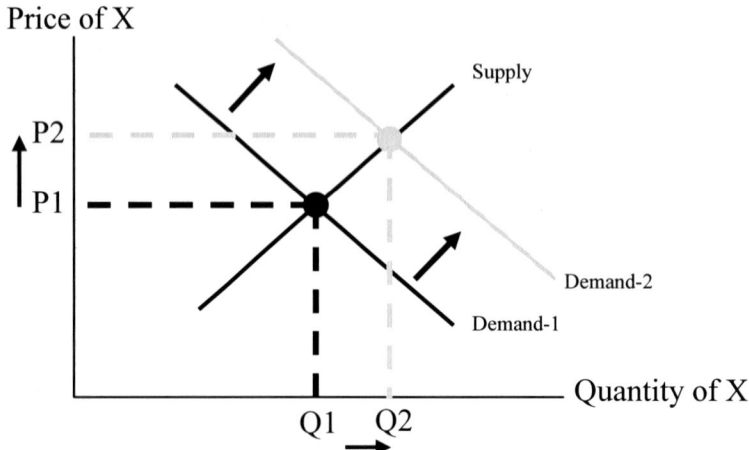

If the market is at equilibrium, a decrease in the demand curve will decrease the equilibrium quantity and the equilibrium price.

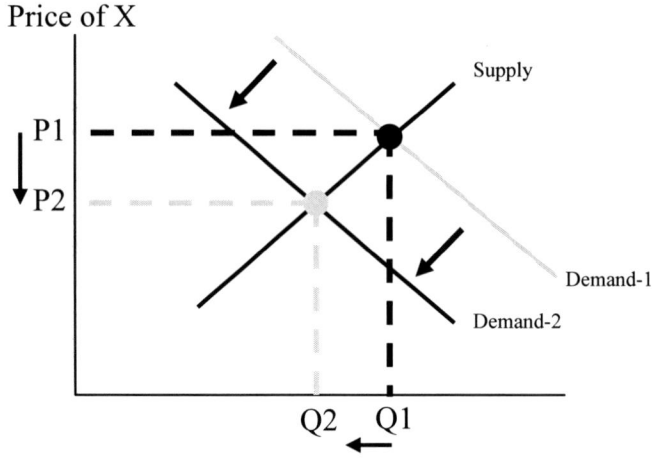

If the market is at equilibrium, an increase in the supply curve will increase the equilibrium quantity and the decrease the equilibrium price.

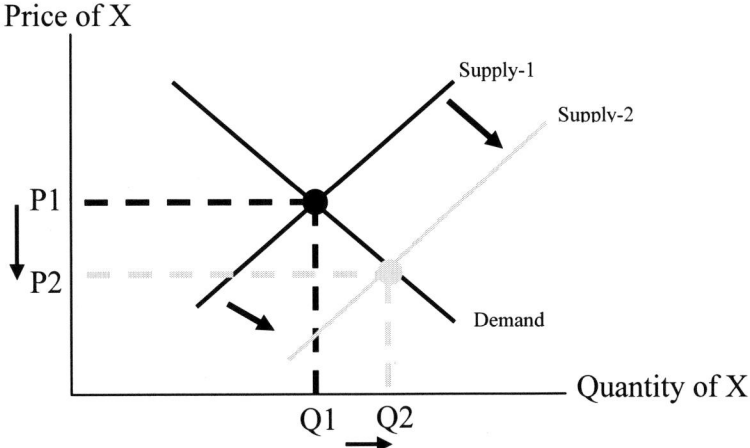

If the market is at equilibrium, a decrease in the supply curve will decrease the equilibrium quantity and increase the equilibrium price.

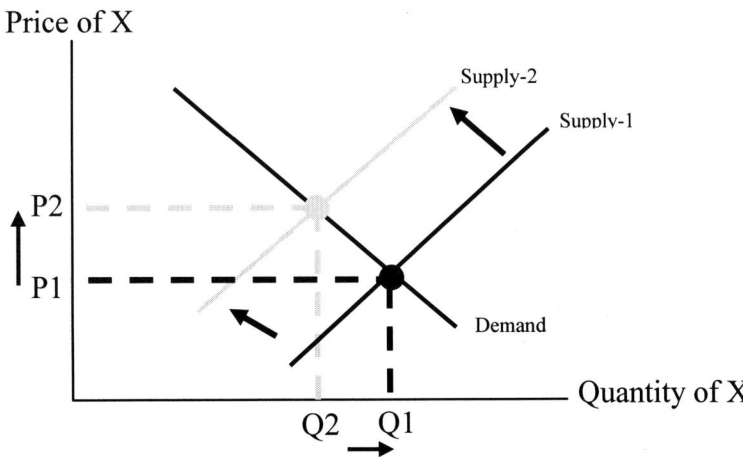

Summary of Supply and Demand

Which curve shifts?	Which direction is the shift?	What happens to the equilibrium price?	What happens to the equilibrium quantity?
Demand	right	increase	increase
Demand	left	decrease	decrease
Supply	right	decrease	increase
Supply	left	increase	decrease
both	right	ambiguous	increase
both	left	ambiguous	decrease
both	Demand right Supply left	increase	ambiguous
both	Demand left Supply right	decrease	ambiguous

Consumer Surplus

I. INTRODUCTION

In our last lesson we introduced the supply and demand model to explain how free markets work. One of the main lessons in that chapter was that prices tend to gravitate toward an equilibrium price and quantity. In this tutorial you will use the same conceptual model to answer a very important question:

Are free markets the best way to distribute society's resources?

A good way to answer this question is by assuming that any distributional outcome that maximizes social welfare, or benefits, should be preferred. Therefore, in order to answer our main question we are going to take a step-by-step process by trying to answer the following three questions:

1. How do economists measure social welfare/benefits?
2. How much social welfare/benefit is generated by free markets?
3. Is it possible to generate more social welfare/benefit by distributing society's resources in a different way?

II. THE EXAMPLE: MARKET FOR ONE-BEDROOM APARTMENTS

To put things in perspective we will use a brand new example for this section: the market for one-bedroom rental apartments around campus town. The area adjacent to a university campus is always full of apartment rentals for those students who decide not to live in the university dorms (usually juniors and seniors).

Every time an apartment is rented (or a market transaction takes place) society's benefits can be divided into two basic groups:

1- The benefits that accrue to the prospective tenant who rent the apartment
2- The benefits that accrue to the landlord.

III. WILLINGNESS TO PAY AND STEP-WISE DEMAND CURVE

Supposed the whole market for one-bedroom apartments was made of four renters: Maria, Roger, Anna, and Jose. After a careful review of their finances these four renters will come up with the most they are **willing to pay** for a one-bedroom apartment. We call this top price a consumer is willing to pay for a good or service the consumer's **willingness to pay**.

The following table lists the willingness to pay for one-bedroom apartments for each of our four renters:

Table 1: Willingness to Pay for one-bedroom apartments

	Willingness to Pay for One-Bedroom Apartment
MARIA	$800
ROGER	$750
ANNA	$700
JOSE	$600

As you can see from the table, Maria is the one with the highest willingness to pay, $800, follow by Roger, $750, then Anna, $700, and finally Jose, $600. This information can also be presented in the same diagram we used for our last tutorial. As you remember that diagram had quantity along the horizontal axis and price along the vertical axis. So, in the case of our apartment example, we would need to use a diagram with quantity of apartments in the horizontal axis and the rent, or price of apartments, in the vertical axis.

Figure 1: Step-wise demand curve for one-bedroom apartments

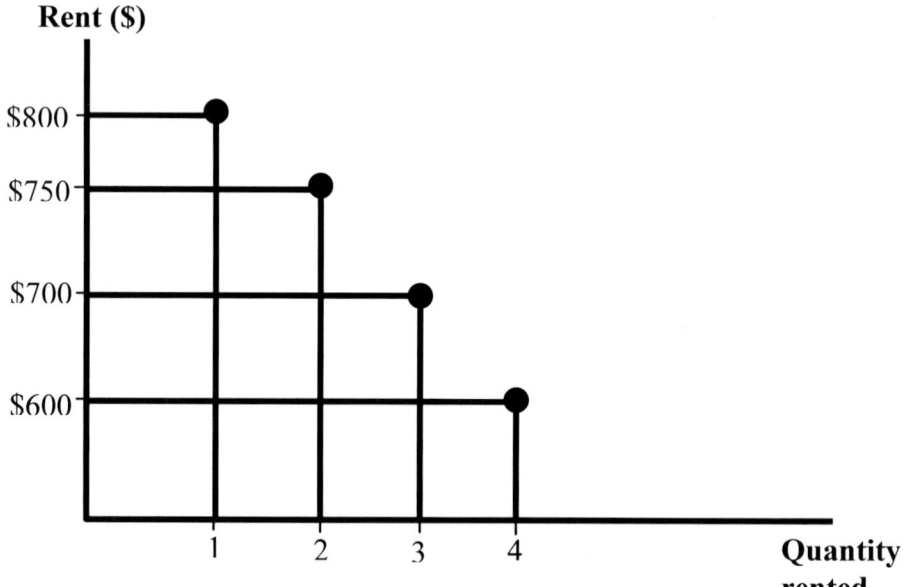

The best way to transfer the information from the table to the diagram is to begin with a high price and see who is willing to buy at that price, then lower the price and see who is willing to buy at that price, and so on and so on. In terms of the diagram, this procedure also allows us to move from left to right along the horizontal axis.

Question: who would be willing to rent apartments at a rent of $800?
Answer: only Maria would be willing to rent an apartment at a rent of $800.

At a rent of $800, only Maria would be willing to rent an apartment. Therefore, our first coordinate would be 1,800; at a rent of 800, only one apartment is rented.

Question: how many apartments would be rented at a rent of $750?

Answer: two apartments: one by Maria and one by Roger.

At a price of $750, two apartments would be rented: one by Maria and one by Roger. So our second coordinate is 2, 750.

Question: how many apartments would be rented at a rent of $700?
Answer: three apartments: one by Maria, one by Roger, and one by Anna.

At a price of $700, three students would be willing to rent an apartment: Maria, Roger, and Anna. Therefore our third coordinate is 3, 700.

Question: how many apartments would be rented at a rent of $600?
Answer: four apartments: one by Maria, one by Roger, one by Anna, and one by Jose.

Finally, at a price of $600, all four students are willing to rent, and so our last coordinate for this small market is 4, 600.

Now all we have to do is connect the dots. One temptation would be to connect all the dots with linear segments, as we did to draw the demand curve in the previous chapter. Nevertheless, there is a fundamental difference between this case and the case in the previous tutorial: in the previous tutorial each coordinate represented the case for a large number of consumers. In this case, each coordinate represent the situation for only ONE consumer. Therefore, we can not connect the dots with linear segments; we must do it in step-wise fashion.

The first horizontal segment goes from 0 to 1 at a height of $800 and represents the first consumer: Maria. The second horizontal segment, from 1 to 2 at a height of $750, represents the second consumer, Roger, and so on and so on.

The resulting curve is still our famous demand curve, since it gives us information about how many apartments are rented at different price.

IV. CONSUMER SURPLUS

Now we are ready to use both the table and the diagram to investigate the benefits these four consumers gain from participating in the market. Let's begin by looking at the table and assuming the rent for apartments were $700. We had already determined that at rent only three renters would be willing to rent: Maria, Roger and Anna. Now let's ask the following question: how much better off these three consumers will be after they rent the one-bedroom apartment for $700?

Question: how much better off Maria, Roger, and Anna will be after thy rent the 1-bedroom apartment for $700?

Answer: If Marie rents the apartment for $700, after the transaction she will be better off by $100 dollars, which is the difference between how much she is willing to pay and how much she actually pays for the apartment. In other words, since Marie is willing to pay $800 a month for an apartment, but she only ends of paying $700, after the transaction takes place she has a left over of $100. This leftover is Maria's **individual consumer surplus**.

Individual Consumer Surplus: Individual consumer surplus is the net gain to an individual buyer from the purchase of a good. It is equal to the difference between the buyer's willingness to pay and the price paid.

On the other hand, Roger would gain a surplus of $50, given his willingness to pay of $750, and Anna would gain a surplus of $0, since her willingness to pay is exactly $700.

Therefore, once we add the consumer surplus for each individual renter we have a **total consumer surplus** of $150. We will call Total Consumer Surplus the sum of the individual consumer surpluses of all the buyers of a good in a market.

Total consumer surplus: is the sum of the individual consumer surpluses of all the buyers of a good in a market.

One important thing to notice is that consumer surplus is a good representation of the benefits renters receives from renting the apartment. For instance, although Maria is not actually putting $100 in cash in her pocket when she rents an apartment for $700, it is as it she was since she now has a place to live and some money leftover after the transaction took place. If nothing else, it should be readily apparent that Maria is happier when she rents an apartment than when she does not. This is the same as saying that Maria receives benefits every time she is able to participate in the market for rental apartments.

Now let's locate the total consumer surplus in the diagram. We already know that the total consumer surplus when the rent is $700 is $150. So all we need to do is to locate that quantity of $150 inside the diagram. Again, let's do this one consumer at a time.

Figure 2: Consumer Surplus for market with four renters

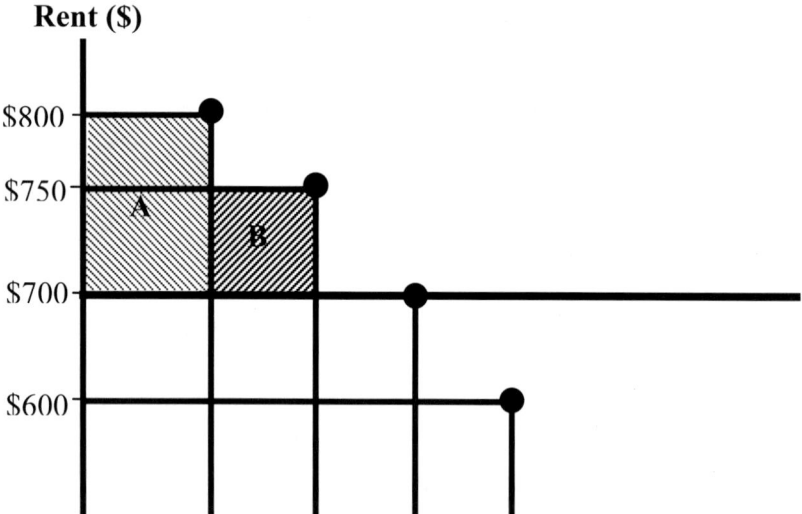

At $700, Maria gains a surplus of $100, since she is willing to pay $800. To find the consumer surplus for Maria in the diagram we look at the most she is willing to pay, which is given by the horizontal segment with height of $800 and length of 1. Since consumer surplus is willingness to pay minus price paid, consumer surplus for Maria must be the space between that segment (her willingness to pay) and the price line; area A in the diagram. To verify that this is in fact correct, let use some basic geometry. Remember that to obtain any area for a rectangle we multiply its height by its length. As we said before, box A has a length of 1, since it represents one consumer, and a height of $100, which is the difference between willingness to pay ($800) and price ($700). So box A has an area equal to $100.

Question: Identify in the diagram the consumer surplus Roger receives from renting an apartment for $700.

Answer: Area B

The second student, Roger, is willing to pay $750, so the second apartment generates a surplus of $50. Again, this is equal to area B, or the area between the demand curve and the price from 1 to 2.

Question: Identify in the diagram the consumer surplus Anna receives from renting an apartment for $700.

Answer: Anna receives no surplus.

Finally, Anna rents an apartment but does not get any surplus since her willingness to pay is the same as the actual price.

So at a price of $700 consumer surplus is equal to the sum for the areas of A and B, which is $150.

Bottom Line

Consumer surplus is always the space between the demand curve and the price line, up to the point of consumption.

V. A DECREASE IN PRICE

Question: What about if the rent for any one-bedroom apartments was $500, instead of $700. Would total consumer surplus increase or decreased with this lower price?

Answer: Consumer surplus increases when the price goes down.

Let's look at the table first. If the rent was $500 Maria would gain $300, Roger would gain $250, Anna $200 and Jose (who is now able to rent an apartment) gains $100 in surplus. So the total surplus in this small market increased to $850! Notice that total consumer increased due to two separate reasons: 1) new consumers enter the market, and 2) the surplus for those renters that were renting before increased.

The diagram shows the same result. When the price goes from $700 to $500 new consumers will enter the market and they will gain some surplus adding to whatever surplus existed before. In the diagram, this is represented by area D, which is the consumer surplus gained by Jose, who at a price of $500 is able to rent an apartment and gain a surplus of $100 (the area of box D).

Figure 3: A Decrease in the Price and Consumer Surplus

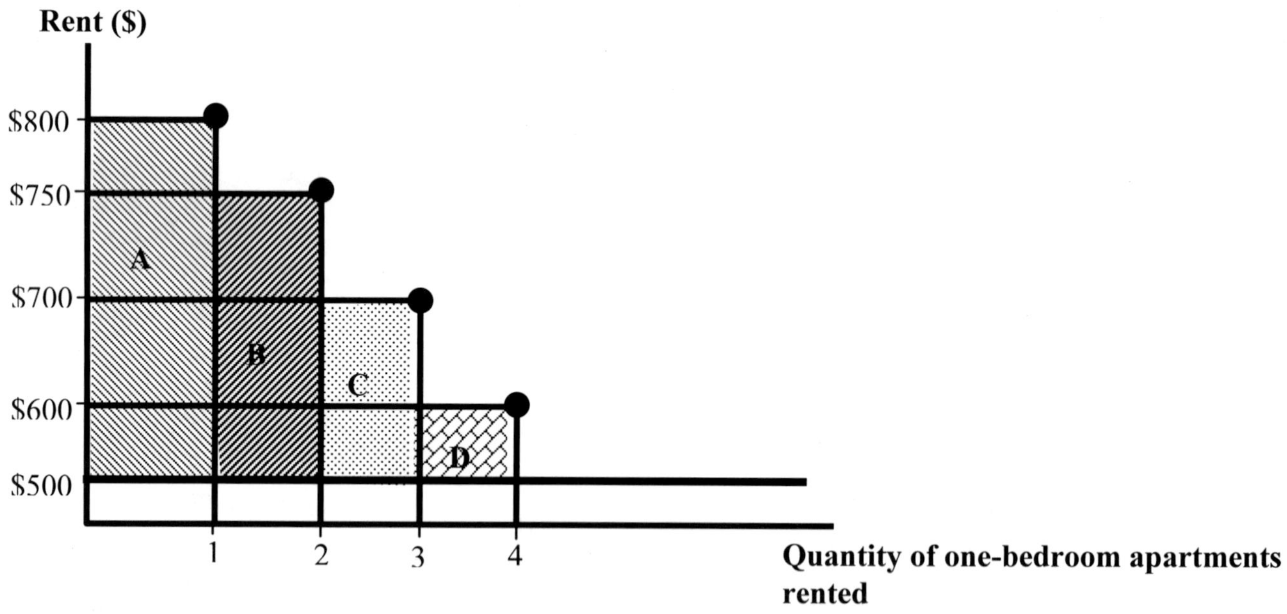

Second, since the price is lower, those consumers that were renting apartments at a higher price before will be able gain even more surplus with the lower price. In the diagram this is represented by the expansion of areas A, the additional consumer surplus gain by Maria, the expansion of area B, the additional surplus gain by Roger, and by area C, the additional surplus gain by Anna (who now is able to gain some surplus).

So now consumer surplus is equal to the sum of areas A, B, C, and D, or $850.

Bottom Line

If the price goes down consumer surplus goes up

VI. AN INCREASE IN PRICE

Question: What about if the rent for any 1-bedroom apartments was $775, instead of $700. Would total consumer surplus increase or decreased with this lower price?

Answer: Consumer surplus goes down.

At that price, only Maria would be willing to rent an apartment, and total consumer surplus would be whatever she is able to gain ($50). Again, total consumer surplus is reduced due to: 1) the fact that some consumers leave the market and hence their surplus is gone along with them, and 2) the surplus for those consumers that are able to stay in the market is lower due to the higher price.

Figure 4: An Increase in the Price and Consumer Surplus

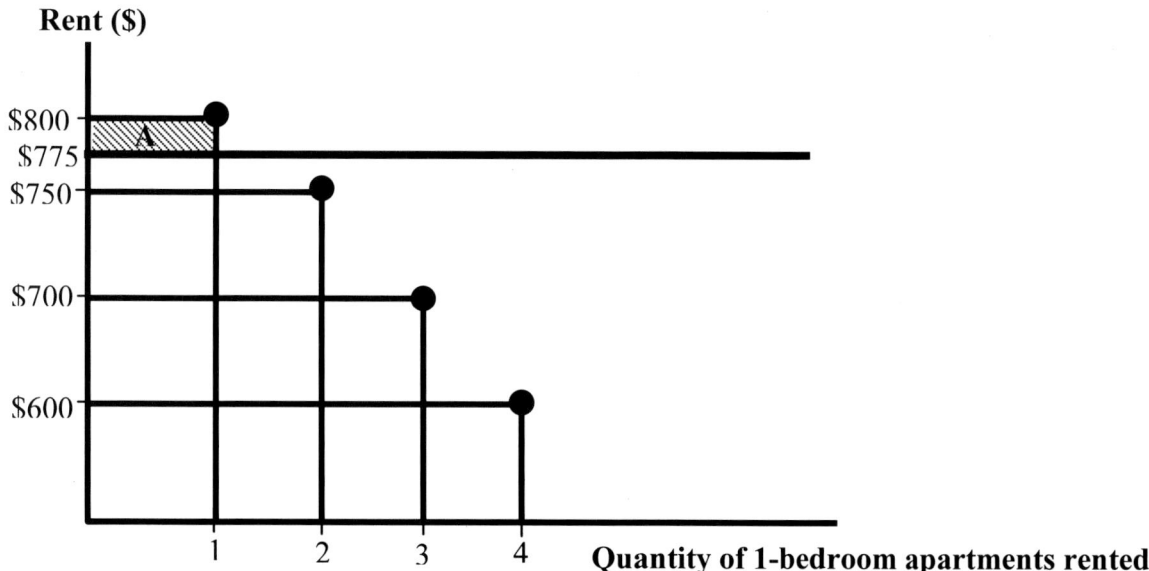

Again, the diagram shows the same result. Since the willingness to pay from any of the consumers has not change, it is clear that the area representing consumer surplus is now smaller that before. And, as it was mentioned before, consumer surplus is smaller due to two reasons:

- First, there is less number of students willing to rent an apartment at $775, compared to $700. Any consumer surplus that was gained by those consumers exiting the market is loss. In the diagram, this is equivalent to the loss of area B, which was the consumer surplus gained by Roger when the price was $700. At $775, since Roger is not willing to rent an apartment, his consumer surplus is gone.

- Second, those consumers that stay in the market will have a smaller leftover after renting the apartment. In the diagram this is equivalent to the shrinkage of area A, which was the consumer surplus Maria was gaining at a price of $700. Since the price of $775 cuts into Maria's surplus, total consumer surplus is reduced.

Bottom Line

If the price goes up consumer surplus goes down.

To summarize, here are the three key points we have developed so far:
1- Consumer surplus is the area between the demand curve and the price line
2- When the price goes up, consumer surplus is reduced.
3- When the price goes down, consumer surplus is increased.

VII. CONSUMER SURPLUS FOR THE WHOLE MARKET

Now that we understand consumer surplus for a small market of four consumers we are ready to extrapolate what we have learned to a larger market composed of thousands of apartments rented each month. Have in mind that nothing in our analysis is going to change when we consider the larger market: the concepts we have developed are the same regardless of the size of the market. The only difference between our example with 4 renters and the general case for the whole market is in terms of the shape of the demand curve. The demand curve for the whole market will look the same as the demand we derived in our previous tutorial; smooth and not step-shaped. The reason for this is due to the fact that each coordinate for this demand curve represents a large number of consumers.

Figure 5: Consumer Surplus with the Market Demand

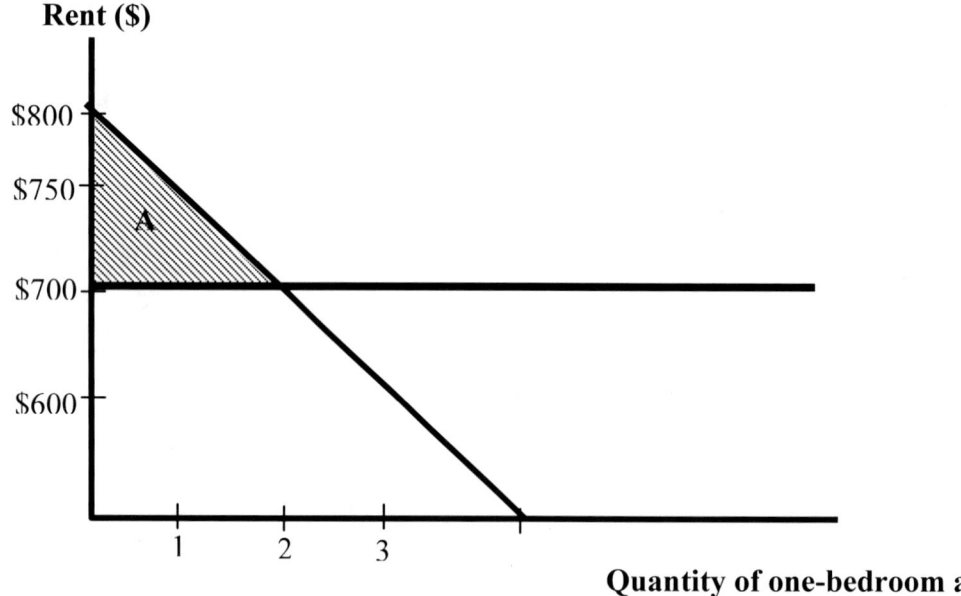

Question: what area in the diagram represents the consumer surplus in the market for apartments if the rent were $700?

Answer:

If the price for any one-bedroom apartment is $700, consumer surplus will be given by the area between the demand curve and the price line, up to 2 thousand apartments, which is the number of apartments that would be rented at this price.

Question: what area in the diagram represents the change in consumer surplus in the market for apartments if the rent goes from $700 to $775?

Figure 6: An Increase in the Price and Consumer Surplus with Market Demand

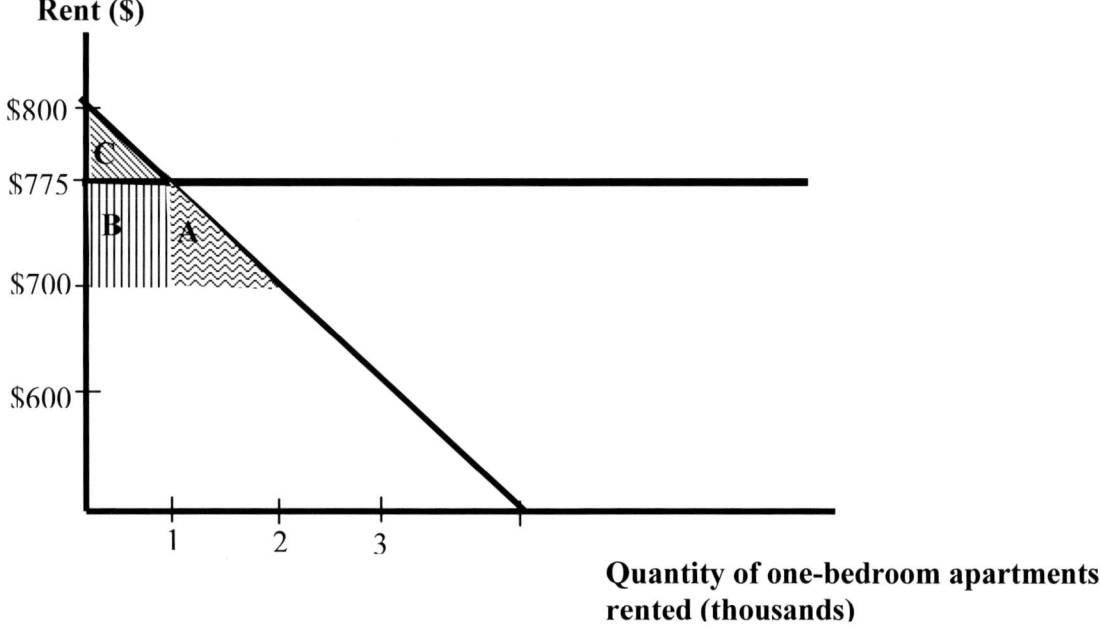

Answer:

What if the price increased? The analysis is exactly the same as when we had only 4 consumers. An increase in the price reduces the number of consumers and hence number of apartments rented from 2 thousand to 1 thousand, and with that all the surplus that was gained when those apartment were rented. That loss of consumer surplus due to renters leaving the market is given by area A in the diagram. Also, consumer surplus is reduced because those renters who are willing to stay in the market will earn less surplus, since the price is now higher. This loss of consumer surplus due to a reduction of surplus to those renters that stay in the market is given by area B. So, when the price increase from $700 to $775 consumer surplus is reduced to area C, which is the same as the original consumer surplus at a rent of $700 minus areas A and B.

Question: what area in the diagram represents the change in consumer surplus in the market for apartments if the rent goes from $700 to $500?

Answer:

What if the price was lower? Again, the analysis is exactly the same as when we had only 4 consumers. A decrease in the price from let say $700 to $500 increases the number of consumers willing to rent and hence the number of apartments rented from 2,000 to 3,000. Those new consumers will earn some surplus, which is an addition to whatever surplus existed when the price was $700. That gain of consumer surplus due to renters entering the market is given by area A in the diagram. Also, consumer surplus is increased because those renters who were willing to stay renting apartments at $700 will earn more surplus with the lower price. The gain of surplus due to an increase in surplus to those renters that were renting before is given by area B. So, when the price goes down from $700 to $500 consumer surplus is increased to area C, which is the same as the original consumer surplus at a rent of $700 plus areas A and B.

Figure 7: An Increase in the Price and Consumer Surplus with Market Demand

Try to complete this diagram on your own.

Elasticity

Modern economics is basically the study of change: specifically: *how consumers and/or producers change their behavior given a change on incentives?* In particular, economists are interest in measuring the ratio of change of one variable in response to a change in another variable. We call that ratio of change the *elasticity*. This tutorial will introduce and explain the following four elasticities:

- Price elasticity of demand
- Income elasticity of demand
- Cross-price elasticity of demand
- Price elasticity of supply.

THE MARKET FOR CIGARETTES

Suppose you were a city government official perusing the goal of reducing teen smoking in your city. One way of accomplishing this would be by increasing the cost of cigarettes by requiring consumers to pay a tax every time they buy a pack of cigarettes. Nevertheless, how much the price would have to increase before having a real effect on teenage consumption of cigarettes? In order to answer this question you would need to know, among other things, how responsive teenagers are to a change in the price of cigarettes. If teenagers' demand for cigarettes is very responsive to changes in the price, then a small increase in the price of cigarettes could have the potential of reducing the rate of teen smoking dramatically. On the other hand, since cigarettes are addictive, their price would have to be increased dramatically before having a real effect on consumption.

Questions such as this one are precisely the one economist try to answer by using the concept of elasticity. So let's continue to use the example of the market for cigarettes in order to demonstrate the concepts fort his lesson.

PRICE ELASTICITY OF DEMAND

What is the price elasticity of demand and how do we calculate it?

The *price elasticity of demand* measures how responsive is the quantity demanded for good X to a change in the price of that good. Specifically,

Price elasticity of demand = percentage change in the quantity demanded of good X / percentage change in the price of X

Formally:

price elasticity of good X = %ΔQ_x / %ΔP_x

where Δ stands for change, Qx stands for quantity demanded of good x and Px stands for the price of good X. So for instance, if the quantity demanded for good X decreases by 10 percent every time the price of X increases by 5 percent the price elasticity of demand is equal to – 2 (-10 / 5).

One very useful tip to calculate elasticities is to know how to calculate percentage changes. Here is a quick and easy formula to do just that (make sure to memorize this formula!).

% Δ X = ((ΔX/X1) x 100) = ((X2 – X1) / X1) x 100

So for instance, let's say X changes from 40 to 60. The percentage of this change would be:

% Δ X = ((X2 – X1) / X1) x 100 = ((60 – 40)/40) x 100 = 50%

Now let's use our formula to solve some problems dealing with our market example: the demand for cigarettes. Suppose you collect some data about consumption of cigarettes at different prices and find out the following demand schedule and demand curve:

Price of Cigarettes ($/pack)	Quantity of Cigarettes Demanded (millions of packs)
$6.00	0
$5.00	5
$4.00	10
$3.00	15
$2.00	20
$1.00	25
$0.00	30

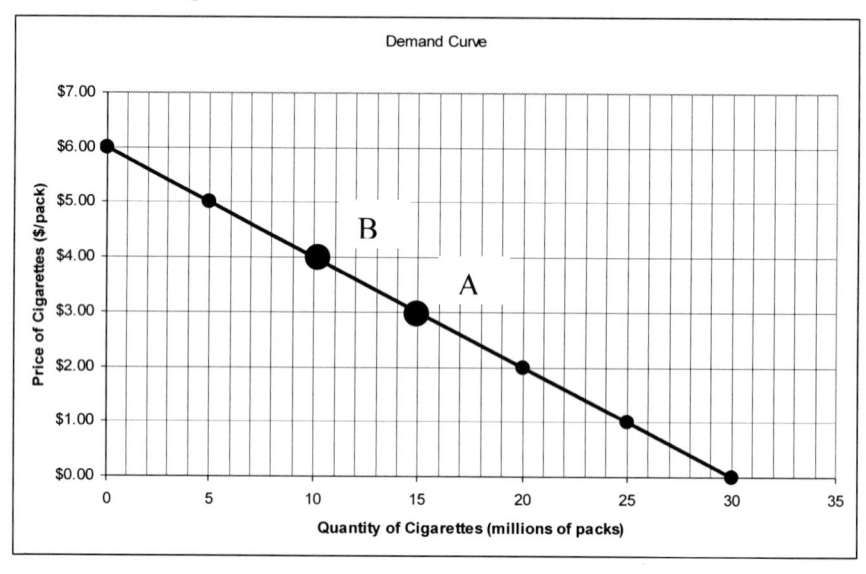

What is the price elasticity of demand when the price of cigarettes goes down from $4 per pack to $3 per pack (segment between A and B in the demand curve)?

Using the formula for elasticity we have that from $4 to $3:

%Δ in price = -25% = ((3 – 4) / 4) x 100

%Δ in quantity = 50% = ((15 – 10) / 10) x 100

price elasticity = %ΔQx / %ΔPx = 50 / 25 = - 2

If you notice, the number for the price elasticity of demand turned out to be negative. This should be no surprise since the Law of Demand says that the quantity demanded is ALWAYS inversely related to the price. Therefore, in order to simplify things, we are going to use the convention of dropping the negative sign from the value of the price elasticity of demand and always report it in absolute (positive) terms. So the price elasticity of demand for cigarettes when the price goes up from $3 to $4 is equal to 2.

How do we classify the price elasticity of demand?

Question:
How responsive is the demand for cigarettes when the price of cigarettes goes down from $4 to $3?

We know the value of the price elasticity of demand, but we still have not determined any criteria for how to classify the responsiveness of the demand for cigarettes. In other words, we can not say that the demand for cigarettes is too responsive or not. For that, we need a set of specific criteria.

We will use the following table to classify the price elasticity of demand:

Value of the Price elasticity of demand is…	We say demand for that good is….	Which means that consumption for that good is…	Because if the price changes by 1 percent, consumption changes by…
> 1	Elastic	Very responsive to price	More than 1 percent
= 1	Unitary	Responsive	Exactly 1 percent
< 1	Inelastic	Not Very responsive to price	Less than 1 percent

Answer:
So we would say that: *when the price of cigarettes goes down from $4 to $3 the demand for cigarettes is elastic since it's value of 2 is larger than 1.*

It is also useful to consider these classifications of elasticity by looking at the extreme cases visually.

One extreme case would be that of a good where a very small change in the price drives the consumption of that good to zero. Economist would say that the demand for that good is *perfectly elastic*. The demand curve for that good would look something like this

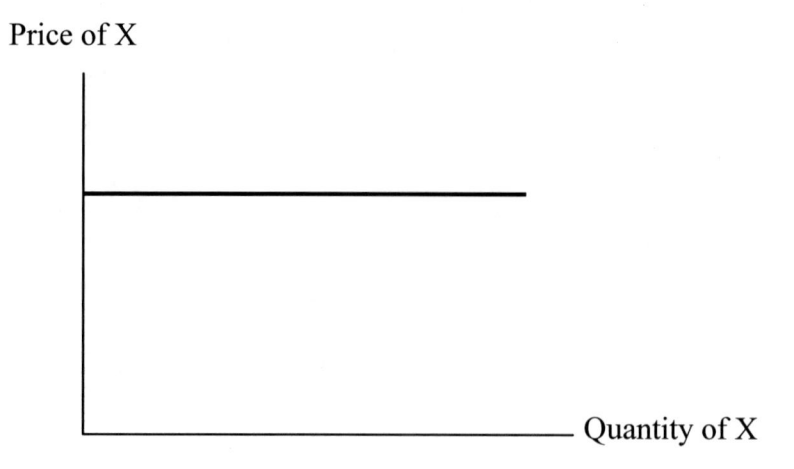

Another extreme case would be that of a good where consumption never changes regardless of any change in price. Economist would say that the demand of that good is *perfectly inelastic*. The demand curve for that good would look something like this.

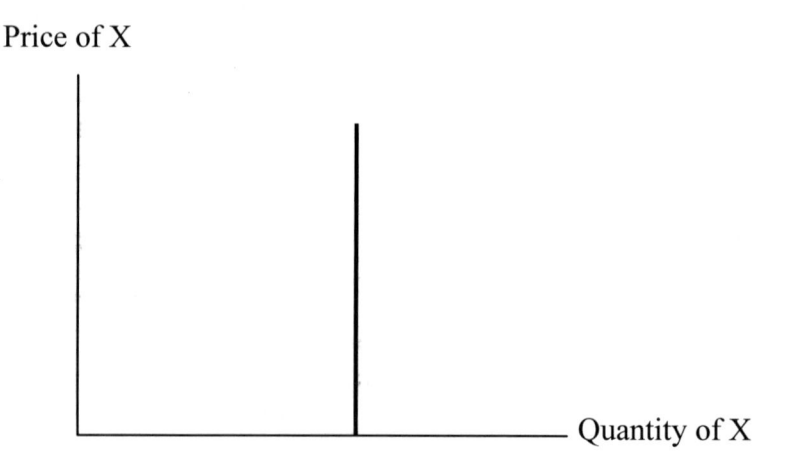

Obviously, most goods will not be either perfectly elastic or perfectly inelastic, but somewhere in the middle. But if you understand the extremes, you will also see there is a relationship between the slope of the demand curve and the price elasticity of demand. In general, the steeper the demand curve is the more Inelastic the demand is and vice versa.

How to calculate the price elasticity of demand more precisely? The mid-point method (optional)

Let's go back to our demand schedule and demand curve and let's try again to calculate the price elasticity of demand of cigarettes between A and B, but this time using the reverse direction: from B to A. Again, using our elasticity equation we have:

%Δ in price = 33% = ((4 – 3) / 3) x 100

%Δ in quantity = -33% = ((10 – 15) / 15) x 100

price elasticity = %ΔQx / %ΔPx = -33 / 33 = - 1 = 1

Notice how different this value is from our previous example; a difference of 100 percent between the two measures! In fact, we would not be able to say that demand is Elastic anymore.

This is a annoying: we would like to have a measure of elasticity that doesn't depend on which way you measure it along a demand curve. In order to correct for this problem, economist use a more elaborated way to calculate specific elasticities called the mid-point method. The mid-point method computes a percentage change by dividing the change by the average (or mid-point) of the initial and final levels. For instance, the average between $4 and $3 is 3.5 (4 + 3 /2). So, according to the mid-point method a change from $4 to $3 should be considered a 29 percent fall since: (3-4)/3.5 x 100 = 29. In the same way, a change from $3 to $4 would be considered a 29 percent rise since: (4-3)/3.5 x 100 = 29.

The same applies to quantity. The mid-point, or average, between 10 and 15 is 12.5 ((10 + 15)/2. So using the mid-point method a change from 10 to 15 should be considered a 40 percent rise since: (15 – 10) / 12.5 x 100 = 40. And a change from 15 to 10 should be considered a 40 percent fall since: (10 – 15) / 12.5 x 100 = -40.

Question: So how does the mid-point method change the calculation of elasticity?

Answer: Well, let's summarize what we discovered about percentage changes when using the mid-point method:

From 4 to 3:
percentage change in Q = 40
percentage change in P = -29

From 3 to 4:
percentage change in Q = 40
percentage change in P = -29

And since the price elasticity is nothing more than the ratio of percentage changes, it is clear that using the mid-point method the price elasticity of demand from A to B would always be equal to 1.4, regardless of the direction we use to calculate it.

Here is a summary of the mid-point method to calculate the price elasticity of demand:

Price elasticity of demand = (X2 – X1)/ [(X1 + X2) /2] / (P2 – P1)/ [(P1 + P2) /2]

So bottom line is:

- The price elasticity of demand is ALWAYS defined as: %ΔQ /%ΔP
- We will ALWAYS report the price elasticity of demand in absolute value (positive).
- To calculate the price elasticity of demand between two points in a demand curve (or demand schedule) we will ALWAYS use the mid-point method.

How does the price elasticity of demand changes along a linear demand curve?

In order to practice, try to complete the following table, which requires you to calculate the price elasticity of demand at different parts of the linear demand curve for cigarettes. When completing the table, remember to use the mid-point method.

Price of Cigarettes ($/pack)	Quantity of Cigarettes Demanded (millions of packs)	Elasticity
$6.00	0	
$5.00	5	
$4.00	10	
$3.00	15	
$2.00	20	
$1.00	25	
$0.00	30	

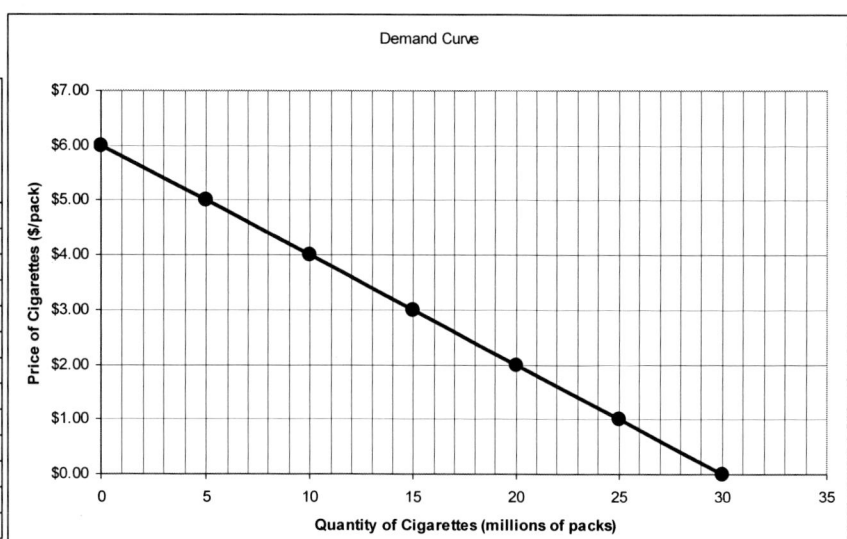

ANSWER

Price of Cigarettes ($/pack)	Quantity of Cigarettes Demanded (millions of packs)	Elasticity
$6.00	0	
		11.00
$5.00	5	
		3.00
$4.00	10	
		1.40
$3.00	15	
		0.71
$2.00	20	
		0.33
$1.00	25	
		0.09
$0.00	30	

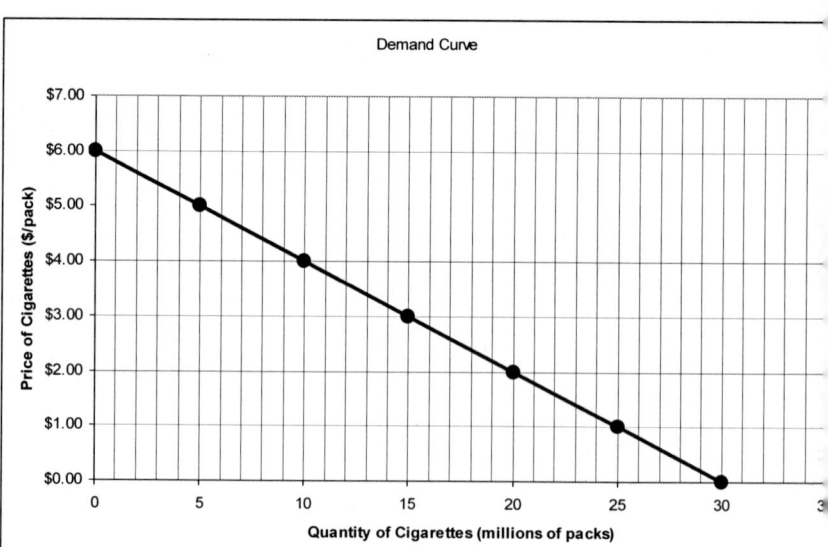

Demand Curve — a linear demand curve plotted from ($0, 30) to ($6, 0) with points at each $1 price increment.

As you can see, the price elasticity of demand gets smaller as you move down the demand curve (or down the rows of the demand schedule). <u>Question:</u> Why do you think this is?

It is best to answer this question intuitively. Consider the price elasticity for something like a candy bar, which is very inexpensive. A change in the price of a candy bar will probably have very little effect over the demand for since your overall budget is not terribly affected by the change in the price (it is hard to imagine you become poorer if the price of Hershey's Kisses go up by 50 percent). Nevertheless, a change in a high-price necessity, such as electricity, would have a much larger impact over your budget and hence your incentive to consume that item or not. In other words, if the price of candy goes up you do not make relevant adjustment to your consumption of candy (Inelastic Demand) but if the price of electricity goes up you will quickly try to adjust your demand for electricity (Elastic Demand). The same idea applies for the demand of any single good. If the price of that good is high, any change in the price would have a dramatic effect over buyers overall budget and they would adapt quickly by changing their consumption. On the other hand, a change in the price when the price is very low has little effect over the overall budget of buyers and hence they do not see the need to adjust their consumption.

Price Elasticity of Demand and the Demand Equation

Surprisingly, there is also a mathematical explanation of why the demand for a good becomes more elastic as you move down a demand curve. In order to understand this, we need to see the relationship between the slope of the demand curve and the elasticity of demand.

Again, the formula for elasticity is:

(1) elasticity = %ΔQx / %ΔPx

Using the formula to derive percentages we said that:

(2) %ΔQ x= ΔQx/Qx
(3) %ΔPx = ΔPx/Px

And combining these two terms into one equation we have:

elasticity = (ΔQx/Qx) / (ΔPx/Px)

or, if we rearrange the terms,

(4) elasticity = (Px/Qx) (ΔQx/ ΔPx)

This equation for elasticity is much more useful. First, notice that the second parenthesis describes the slope of the line with Px on the horizontal axis and Qx on the vertical axis. Hey, but isn't this the inverse of the usual demand curve? Indeed it is! The traditional demand curve is a curve along the xy plane where Qx along the horizontal (x) axis and Px along the vertical (y) axes. So the term (ΔQx/ΔPx) is the inverse of the slope of the demand curve. More formally:

(5) (ΔQx/ΔPx) = 1/slope of demand curve

Now, if we substitute (5) into (4) we have:

(6) elasticity = (Px/Qx) (1/slope of demand curve)

I know, you are probably thinking: "What is the point of all this math?" Well, we have established a direct connection between the price elasticity of demand and the slope of the demand curve. Notice that for some fixed levels of Px and Qx if the slope of the demand curve increases then elasticity decreases and vice versa. This means that other things equal the steeper the demand the demand curve the more Inelastic the demand will be and vice versa.

Now, equation (6) also illustrates another important economic application. Notice that along a fixed demand curve, the larger Px is relative to Qx, the larger the value of elasticity and hence the more Elastic the demand will be. In other words, the elasticity of demand will be different along a linear demand curve, which is what we had set out to demonstrate.

What is the relationship between elasticity of demand and total revenue?

Consider again our initial policy issue: that of reducing teenage smoking. But this time let's consider the policy from the perspective of cigarette sellers. Suppose the government decides to levy the tax on cigarette sellers. A possible way a cigarette company would deal with this tax would be by increasing the price of cigarettes and hence effectively "passing" the tax to the consumers. Nevertheless, in deciding to adopt this policy this company would need to know how elastic demand cigarettes is to changes in the price of cigarettes. More specifically, the company needs to know the effect the increase in the price of cigarettes will have over the revenue it makes from selling cigarettes. On the one hand total revenue could increase, since they are now selling cigarettes at a higher price. Nevertheless, if the reduction in sales is dramatic, the positive effect from the increase in price could be offset by the reduction in sales and total revenue could end up going down. Therefore, it would be nice if the company could anticipate the effect of the change in price over total revenue. As it turns out, it could, by looking at the price elasticity of demand for cigarettes.

In order to understand the relationship between total revenue and elasticity, let's again go back to our demand schedule and demand curve. This time, let's concentrate on the total revenue sellers of cigarettes make at every price and quantity combinations.

Price of Cigarettes ($/pack)	Quantity of Cigarettes Demanded (millions of packs)	Total Revenue	Change in Total Revenue	Elasticity
$6.00	0	$0.00		
			$25.00	11.00
$5.00	5	$25.00		
			$15.00	3.00
$4.00	10	$40.00		
			$5.00	1.40
$3.00	15	$45.00		
			-$5.00	0.71
$2.00	20	$40.00		
			-$15.00	0.33
$1.00	25	$25.00		
			-$25.00	0.09
$0.00	30	$0.00		

Two patterns are evident from looking at the table. First, the total revenue goes up and then down as the price of cigarettes is reduced. But to understand this pattern we need first to explain the other obvious pattern, which has to do with the relationship between the change in total revenue (column 4) and elasticity (column 5). If you compare the last two columns you will notice that when demand is elastic the change in total revenue to an increase in the price is positive. On the other hand, when demand is Inelastic an increase in the price reduces total revenue. Question: Why is this?

Well, consider the definition of total revenue.

Total revenue is the number of units sold times the price of each unit. Formally,

Total Revenue = Price x Quantity = P x Q

When the price of cigarettes goes up, each of the two variables in the total revenue equation change in opposite direction: P goes up but Q goes down. The ultimate effect the change in price has on total revenue depends on which of the two variables changes by more.

If the variable Q goes down more than the variable P goes up, total revenue goes down. And this is exactly what would happen when the demand is elastic; since the negative change in Q is proportionally larger than the change in P.

On the other hand, if the positive change in P is proportionally larger than the negative change in Q, total revenue will go up. And this is exactly what happens when the demand is Inelastic, since a proportional change in Q is lower to a change in P.

So to summarize, we have the following:

If demand is ….	an increase in price will….	and a decrease in price will…
Elastic (>1)	Decrease Total Revenue	Increase Total Revenue
Unitary (=1)	Does not change Total Revenue	Does not change Total Revenue
Inelastic (<1)	Increase Total Revenue	Decrease Total Revenue

INCOME ELASTICITY OF DEMAND

The income elasticity of demand measures how responsive quantity demanded is to changes in the average income of the consumer. Formally,

Income Elasticity of Demand = %ΔQx / %ΔI

Notice that all we have done here is again replaced the P for I in the elasticity equation. But the idea of elasticity is the same, now we are just applying it to income. One important difference, however, is that the sign of this elasticity may or may not be positive. For a normal good, where an increase in income causes an increase in demand, the income elasticity of demand will have a positive sign. Nevertheless, for an inferior good, where an increase in income causes a decrease in demand, the income elasticity of demand will be negative.

CROSS-PRICE ELASTICITY OF DEMAND

The cross-price elasticity of demand measures how responsive the demand for good X is to a change in the price of related good Y. Formally,

Cross-Price Elasticity of Demand = %ΔQx / %ΔPy

Again, notice that all we did was to replace the Py for Px from the original elasticity equation. Also remember that for this elasticity the sign is also relevant since it may not always be positive.

For complementary goods, where an increase in the price of y causes a decrease in the demand for x, the sign of the cross-price elasticity will be negative. On the other hands, for goods that are substitutes, where an increase in the price of y causes an increase in the demand for x, the cross price elasticity of demand will be positive.

THE PRICE ELASTICITY OF SUPPLY

If you understand the price elasticity of demand, then understanding the price elasticity of supply is really a piece of cake.

Definition and Formula/Equation

The *price elasticity of supply* measures how responsive is the quantity supplied for good X is to a change in the price of that good. Formally, the equation for this elasticity is given by the following equation:

price elasticity of supply for good X = %ΔQx / %ΔPx

where Δ stands for change, Qx stands for quantity supplied of good X and Px stands for the price of good x. So for instance, if the quantity suplied for good x increases by 10 percent every time the price of x increases by 5 percent the price elasticity of demand is equal to 2. Which, again, means that a 1 percent increase in the price of x causes a 2 percent increase in the price of Y.

One thing to notice is that price elasticity of supply is ALWAYS going to be positive, since the quantity supplied always increases with price.

Classifying the Price Elasticity of Supply

So can we already the following question: how responsive is the supply for cigarettes to a change in the price of cigarettes? Again, we can not say that the supply for cigarettes is too responsive or not. For that, we need a set of specific criteria.

We will use the following table to classify the price elasticity of supply:

Value of the Price elasticity of demand is…	We say demand for that good is….	Which means that consumption for that good is…	Because if the price changes by 1 percent, consumption changes by…
> 1	Elastic	Very responsive to price	More than 1 percent
= 1	Unitary	Responsive	Exactly 1 percent
< 1	Inelastic	Not Very responsive to price	Less than 1 percent

One extreme case would be that of a good where a very small change in the price drive the consumption of that good to zero. Economist would say that the price elasticity of supply for that good is perfectly elastic. The supply curve for that good would look something like this (insert diagram with Perfectly Elastic Curve).

Another extreme case would be that of a good where quantity sold never changes, regardless of any change in price. Economist would say that the price elasticity of supply for that good is perfectly Inelastic. The supply curve for that good would look something like this (insert diagram with Perfectly Inelastic Curve).

Obviously, most goods will not be either perfectly elastic or perfectly inelastic, but somewhere in the middle. But, if you understand the extremes, you will also see there is a relationship between the slope of the supply curve and the price elasticity of supply. In general the steeper the supply curve is the more inelastic the supply is and vice versa.

Production

I. INTRODUCTION

This lesson introduces two main topics: 1) the process by which a firm converts inputs such as labor and capital into output, and 2) an analysis of some important cost measures associated with this production process.

The principles we will explained here apply to any production process, from a company producing and selling widgets, to a student producing answers for an economic exam. But, in the interest of simplicity, we will focus on one particular example: the production of haircuts. Cleancuts is a unisex hair salon on campus town serving mostly students. They specialize in offering hair grooming services that are affordable, fast and high-quality. Although they offer many different types of services (in addition to selling hair products) we are going to concentrate on their most popular service: the basic haircut.

II. INPUTS OF PRODUCTION
a. Labor and Capital

Question: What kinds of inputs are needed to produce a haircut?
Answer: Labor (hairdressers), barber chair, scissors, etc.

What do you think are the inputs Cleancuts uses in order to produce a haircut? See if you can list at least three of these inputs.

To name a few, the following inputs are probably needed in order to produce a haircut:
- Labor (hairdresser)
- A barber chair
- scissors, clippers and other hair grooming instruments
- water
- hair products
- electricity
- rent

We can categorize these different types of inputs in two broad categories: labor and capital.

Question: which one of these inputs would be considered "labor"? Which ones would be consider "capital"?
Answer: a bracket is placed to differentiate the two set of inputs.

b. Fixed Inputs and Variable Inputs

Another way to divide the inputs has to do with how easy or hard it would be to change them. For instance, consider hairdressers. Economists call this input a variable input, since it is an input whose quantity the firm can vary at any time. This is in contrast to barber chairs, which would take more time to purchase and get rid of off. These types of inputs are call fixed inputs.

Variable inputs: an input whose quantity the firm can vary at any time.
Fixed inputs: an input whose quantity is fixed for a period of time and cannot be varied.

Question: what other inputs could be considered fixed for Cleancuts' production process? What other inputs could be considered variable?

Answer:
   Fixed: rent, cash registers, counters, etc.
   Variable: water, electricity, etc.

Labor will be anything related to human inputs; in the case of the hair saloon example, labor will be made of hairdressers. All other inputs will be considered capital.

III. THE PRODUCTION FUNTION

To serve every customer Cleancuts basically combines all these inputs to provide one haircut for every customer. The process could be imagined in the following way.

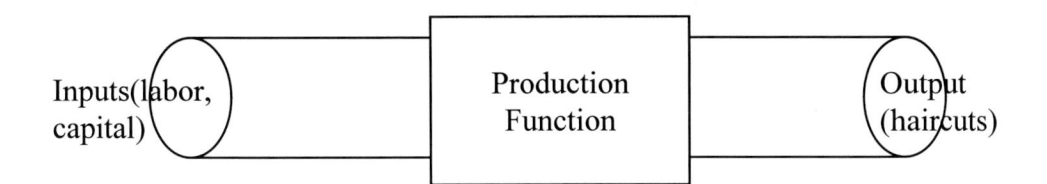

Inputs(labor, capital) → Production Function → Output (haircuts)

In this tutorial we will concentrate mostly on the square in the middle: we call this the "production function."

Production function: the relationship between the quantity of inputs a firm uses and the quantity of output it produces.

In order to understand the production of haircuts better, let us concentrate on the use one particular input: hairdressers (labor). Also, for the time being, let's assume Cleancuts is stuck with one barber chair (capital) and is not able to increase or decrease the number of them. In other words, we will assume that hairdressers are the only variable input and barber chairs the only fixed input. The following table gives an approximation of the number of haircuts Cleancuts can provide per hairdresser working that day (again, assuming one barber chair):

Table 1: The Production Function

Labor (quantity of hairdressers/day)	Output (quantity of haircuts/day)	Marginal Product
0	0	
		5
1	5	
		7
2	12	
		9
3	21	
		7
4	28	
		5
5	33	
		3
6	36	
		1
7	37	

As we have stressed throughout most of these tutorials, economists are mostly concerned with how variables change, an in terms of the production function this change has to do with the rate at which output changes as labor is increase. This rate of change is called: *the marginal product of labor*, and it's given in the third column of the table above. Its formal equation is given by:

Marginal Product of Labor = change in the quantity of output / change in the quantity of labor.

Marginal product of an input: is the additional quantity of output that is produced by using one more unit of that input.

Let's think about what is happening. The first hairdresser hired will be able to finish 5 haircuts in one eight-hour shift. This seems like a small number, but given the fact this hairdresser will have to attend to the cash register, in addition to cutting hair, her productivity of haircuts will not be as high as possible. The second worker, therefore, adds considerable amount of haircuts to the production process given the fact that with two employees there is room for more specialization: one person cuts the hair while the other one attends to the register. Nevertheless, a third worker will not add as much output as the second: can you think why?

Question: Why the fourth worker does not add as much output as the third worker?

Answer: the answer has to do with what economics called: *diminishing returns to an input,* which is when an increase in the quantity of an input, holding the levels of all other inputs fixed, leads to a decline in the marginal product of that input.

Diminishing returns to an input: when an increase in the quantity of an input, holding the levels of all other inputs fixed, leads to a decline in the marginal product of that input.

If we think of the situation at the hair salon it should not be difficult to understand why the marginal product of the third worker is lower than the marginal product of the second: the number of barber chairs is fixed! With only one chair and three hairdressers there will be some idle time where one (or more) of the workers will have to wait for a barber chair to become available. This problem becomes more severe as more and more workers are added.

Now let's transfer the information into our usual xy plane, with the quantity of labor in the horizontal axis and the quantity of output in the vertical axis. The resulting diagram is known as the total product curve.

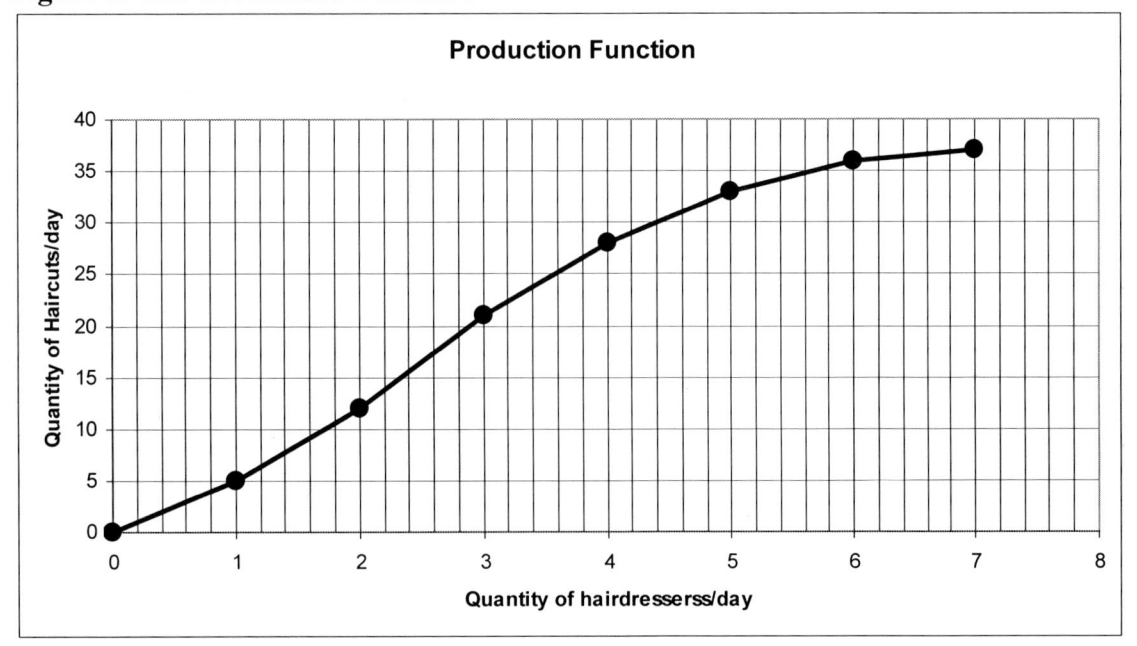

Figure 1: The Production Function

The total product curve: shows how the quantity of output depends on the quantity of the variable input, for a given quantity of the fixed input.

The slope of this curve will be given by the change in output divided by change in labor, which, as we explained above, is also known as the marginal product of labor. Notice how this slope increases with small number of employees reaches a peak and then decreases. Can you tell why?

Question: why does the total product curve increases at decreasing rates?
Answer: because of the diminishing marginal returns to the input.

Careful!
Also, notice that although the marginal product of labor eventually decreases with more output, the change in output is always positive!

Question: what would happen to the marginal product of labor and the total product curve if Cleancuts acquires an extra barber chair?

Answer: the curve will shift up.

Another chair will allow employees to stop from crowding the chairs, and hence all workers will be able to increase their production. The effects of this can be seen as a shift up of the total product curve. The opposite will happen if the number of chairs is reduced.

Bottom Line

- Production inputs can be divided into variable and fixed inputs.
- All inputs will, at some point, exhibit diminishing marginal returns.
- An increase in the fixed input will allow the marginal product of the other inputs to increase.

IV. THE COSTS OF PRODUCTION
a. Variable Costs and Fixed Costs

Since there are two types of inputs, variable and fixed, there will also be two types of costs associated with producing haircuts. The costs associated with the variable inputs are called: variable costs. The costs associated with the fixed inputs are called: fixed costs. The total fixed costs of production are then the addition of the variable costs and the fixed costs. Formally:

Total Costs = TC = Variable Costs + Fixed Costs = VC + FC

A fixed cost is a cost that does not depend on the quantity of output produced. It is the cost of the fixed input.
A variable cost is a cost that depends on the quantity of output produced. It is the cost of the variable input.
The total cost of producing a given quantity of output is the sum of the fixed cost and the variable cost of producing that quantity of output.

b. The Total Cost Curve

For now, let's assume that Cleancuts pays each employee a wage of $80 per day, and that each chair cost about $50 per day. The distribution of variable costs and fixed cost for Cleancuts are given by the following table.

Also, the total cost could be place in a diagram with output on the horizontal axis and cost on the vertical axis.

Table 2: The Costs Production Function

Labor (quantity of hairdressers/day)	Output (quantity of haircuts/day)	Variable Costs	Fixed Costs	Total Costs	Marginal Costs
0	0	$0.00	$50.00	$50.00	
					$16.00
1	5	$80.00	$50.00	$130.00	
					$13.33
2	11	$160.00	$50.00	$210.00	
					$16.00
3	16	$240.00	$50.00	$290.00	
					$26.67
4	19	$320.00	$50.00	$370.00	
					$40.00
5	21	$400.00	$50.00	$450.00	
					$80.00
6	22	$480.00	$50.00	$530.00	
					$80.00
7	23	$560.00	$50.00	$610.00	

Two important things to point out about this total cost curve.

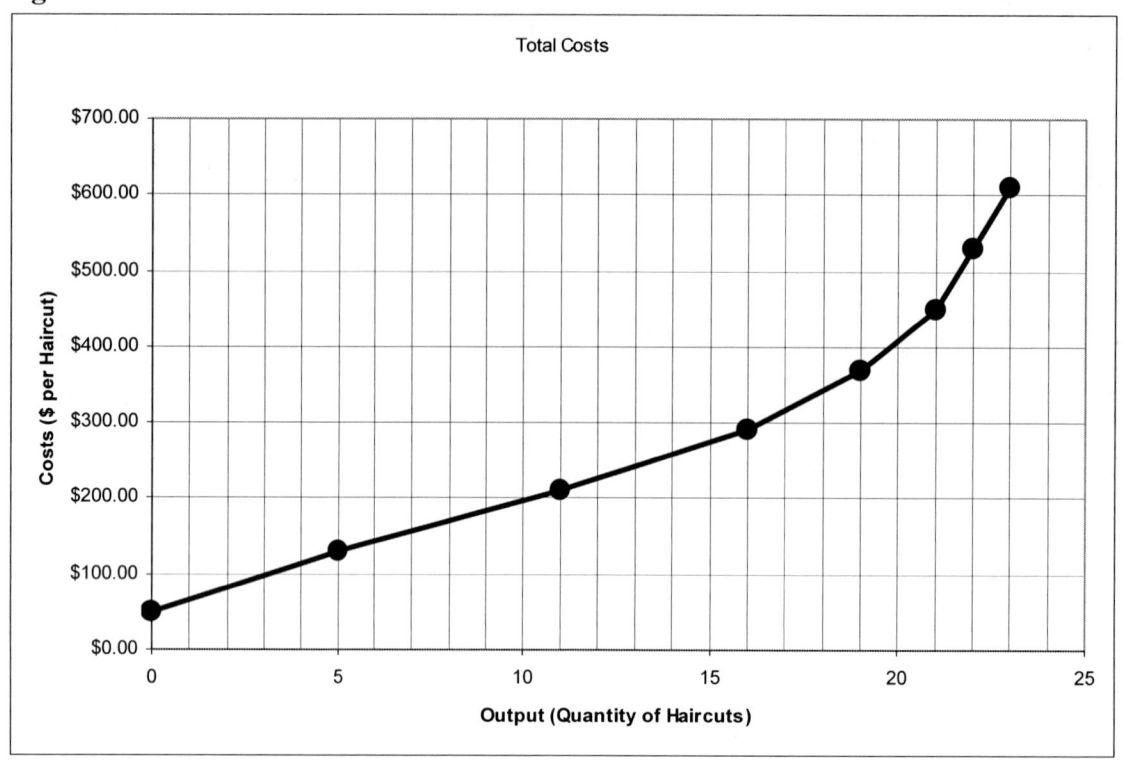

Figure 2: The Total Costs Curve

[Graph showing Total Costs curve: x-axis is Output (Quantity of Haircuts) from 0 to 25, y-axis is Costs ($ per Haircut) from $0.00 to $700.00. The curve starts near $50 at 0 output, rises gradually to about $130 at 5, $210 at 11, $290 at 16, $370 at 19, $450 at 21, $530 at 22, and $610 at 23, showing an increasingly steep slope.]

First, let's compare the shape of the total cost curve with the shape of the total product curve we had developed in the previous section. Do you notice anything interesting about the shape of the two curves?

Question: what do you notice about the shape of the total product curve and the total cost curve?

Answer: They are both mirror images of each other.

If you look carefully, the total product curve and the total cost curve are mirror images of each other. Can you explain why?

Question: why are the total product curve and the total cost curve mirror images of each other?

Answer: because they are both directly influenced by the marginal product of labor.

The answer has to do with the marginal product of labor, which is the concept driving the shape of both curves. Let's explain.

Consider the way the total cost curve is constructed in relation to the total product curve. To construct the total cost curve we are basically taking the output, which is placed in the vertical axis for the total product curve, and placing it on the horizontal axis. Then, we are taking the number of employees, which was originally placed in the horizontal axis for the total product curve, multiplying it by the wage (which is a constant variable) adding the fixed costs (which is also a constant number) and placing it on the vertical axis. So in essence, both curves could be considered to contain the same information organize in a different way!

What is more important, both curves are still directly depending on the marginal product of labor. For instance, consider again how the total cost curve would change if Cleancuts was able to purchase a second barber chair.

Question: how the total cost curve would change if Cleancuts was able to purchases a second chair?

Answer: the total cost curve would shift to the right.

c. Marginal Costs

The second important thing to point out about the total cost curve has to do with the slope of the curve. The equation for the slope of the total cost curve is called the marginal cost and it is also given by the last column of the table above.

The equation for marginal costs is:

marginal costs = MC = change in total costs / change in quantity

And, as we stated above, this slope will be directly related to the marginal product of labor. To see this, consider that:

change in total costs = change in variable cost
change in quantity = marginal product of labor

MC = change in variable cost / marginal product of labor

change in variable cost = wage per employee

MC = wage per employee / marginal product of labor

So, for instance, when Cleancuts decides to hire its first worker, the marginal costs associated with that worker are $16 (80/5 = 16). The second worker adds 6 additional haircuts, and costs another $80, hence the marginal costs at the stage are $13.33 (80/6). Notice that eventually, since the additional output brought by each worker is bound to go down, yet each worker continues to be paid the same wage, the marginal costs of production are going to skyrocket. For instance, the sixth worker adds only one additional haircut, yet she still gets paid $80! So the marginal costs of that worker are $80!

Bottom Line

- Total costs are made up off fixed costs (do not vary with output) and variable costs (vary with output).
- Marginal costs are directly related with the marginal product of the variable input.
- Marginal costs eventually increase with more output due diminishing marginal returns to the input.

d. Average Costs

While understanding the dynamics of the total costs of production is very important, a more revealing cost measure would be done on a per-unit basis. Therefore, it is important we also understand some basic dynamics of different average cost measures. We can calculate the per-unit fixed and variable costs for any production process by dividing each cost measure by the quantity. The resulting measures are called the average fixed costs and average variable costs respectably.

Table 3: The Average Costs Production Function

Labor (quantity of hairdressers/day)	Output (quantity of haircuts/day)	Marginal Costs	Average Variable Costs	Average Fixed Costs	Average Total Costs
0	0				
		$16.00			
1	5		$16.00	$10.00	$26.00
		$13.33			
2	11		$14.55	$4.55	$19.09
		$16.00			
3	16		$15.00	$3.13	$18.13
		$26.67			
4	19		$16.84	$2.63	$19.47
		$40.00			
5	21		$19.05	$2.38	$21.43
		$80.00			
6	22		$21.82	$2.27	$24.09
		$80.00			
7	23		$24.35	$2.17	$26.52

Let's again place these costs measures in the xy plane and see if we can point out some generalities about the shape of these different cost measures.

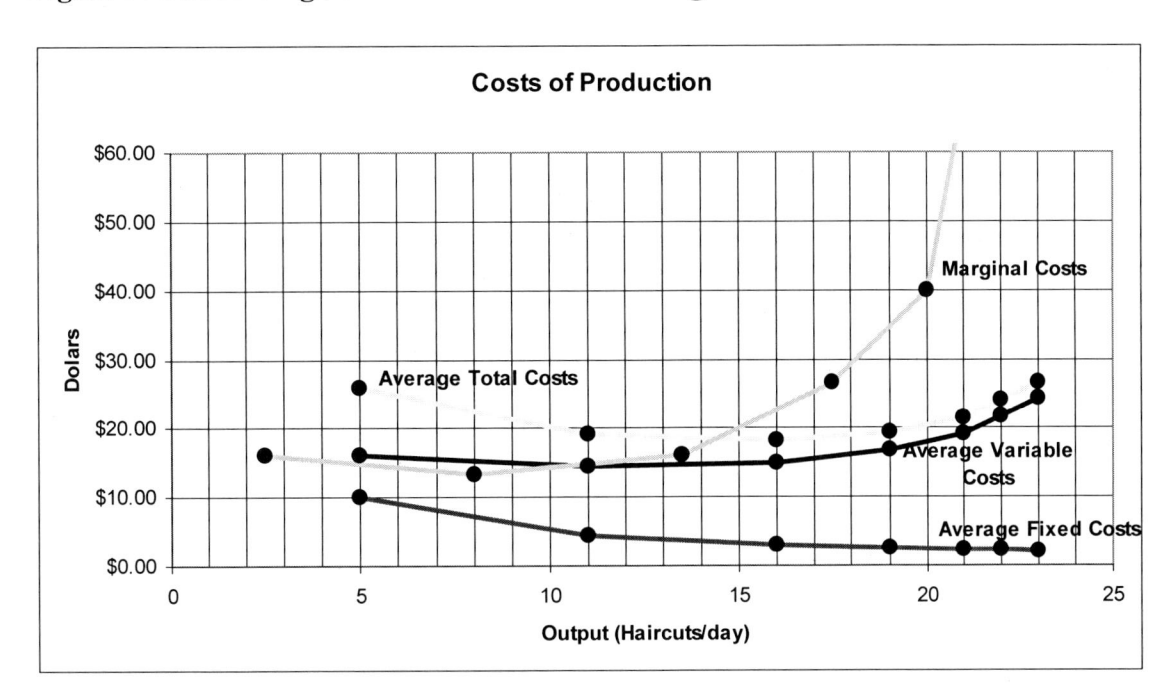

Figure 3: The Average Costs Curves and the Marginal Cost Curve

[Graph: Costs of Production — shows Marginal Costs, Average Total Costs, Average Variable Costs, and Average Fixed Costs curves plotted against Output (Haircuts/day) from 0 to 25 on x-axis and Dollars from $0.00 to $60.00 on y-axis.]

Question: why does the average fixed cost curve always decrease with more output?
Answer: Because fixed costs are fixed as output increases!

Since the fixed costs are fixed, every time we move to the right along the horizontal axis (increase the quantity) the average fixed costs will go down, hence the shape of the average fixed costs curve will always have a decreasing slope.

Question: why does the average variable cost eventually increases with more output?
Answer: Because of diminishing marginal returns to the variable input

The variable costs, on the other hand, do change with output. But, as we explained earlier, the main reason they change has to do with the marginal product of the variable input, which in the case of Cleancuts is the labor. As we hire more and more workers the additional product contributed by each additional worker will go down, yet what we pay those workers remain the same, hence the cost per unit of hiring those workers must eventually go up.

Question: why does the average total cost eventually increases with more output?
Answer: Because of diminishing marginal returns to the variable input

Finally, if we add the average variable costs and the average fixed costs we come up with the average total cost of production. The shape of this curve should also be U-shaped. Can you think of why?

Again, when the quantity is low (or when we have a low number of workers) each additional worker adds a considerable amount of output; hence the cost per unit of output must be rather low at that point. Nevertheless, as we continue to increase workers and hence increase output, each additional worker adds very little additional output but continue to draw the same wage hence the average total cost increase.

e. Marginal Costs and Average Costs

Let's concentrate for a moment on two curves: the average total costs and the marginal cost curves. Do you notice anything particularly interesting about the relationship of these two curves?

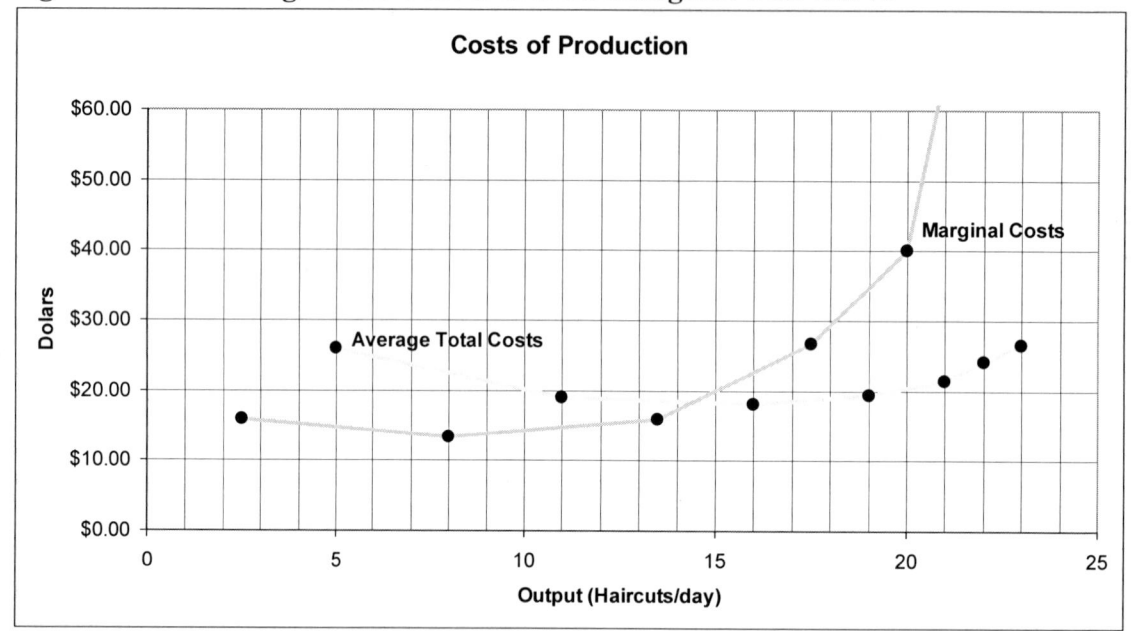

Figure 3: The Average Costs Curves and the Marginal Cost Curve

Question: do you notice something interesting about the relationship of the average total cost curve and the marginal cost curve?

Answer: the marginal cost curve crosses the average total cost curve at the lowest point of the average total cost curve.

Why do you think this is?

Question: why does the marginal cost curve cross the average total cost curve at the lowest point of the average total cost curve?

Answer: because if marginal cost are lower than the average total cost the average cost will decrease and vice versa.

This is simply a mathematical property between marginal and average variables. For instance, consider what happens to your average grade every time you receive a grade for one additional (marginal) examination. If your average before the examination was lower than the grade you obtain in the examination, your class average increases after the examination. On the other hand, if the grade you obtain in your examination is lower than the average grade you had, your average grade will go down.

PART II

CLASS ACTIVITIES

ECON 102   Name: Kaitlyn Lagesse

Prof. Jose Vazquez-Cognet   TA: BQ3
                                                    F: 10-10:50

Classroom Activity: Two Important Economic Principles

Discuss each of the following questions with your partner and then write a few sentences for each of them. I will only collect one sheet for each group. Use the other side for your answers.

A. The Cost-Benefit Principle and the Wonderful Invisible Hand

1. You are an energy-conservation-minded consumer whose only goal in choosing a car is to minimize the extent to which you deplete the planet's store of fossil fuels. You usually drive an average of 7,000 miles every year. If you can't afford to rent a new car, should you rent a 10-year-old Buick ($100/yr, 20 miles per gallon) or a 10-year-old Toyota ($300/yr, 40 mpg)? *To make things simple, assume the price of gasoline is $1/gallon.*

Buick: $100 + \frac{7000}{20} = \$450$

Toyota: $300 + \frac{7000}{40} = \$475$

Toyota b/c for only $25 you conserve gas

* Buick b/c costs less and no one who drives more than you will choose the Buick. If you don't drive the Buick someone else will — if you drive Buick, less gas used overall.

ECON 102   Name: Kaitlyn Lagesse

Prof. Jose Vazquez-Cognet   TA: BQ3
                                    F 10-10:50

Classroom Activity: Two Important Economic Principles

Discuss each of the following questions with your partner and then write a few sentences for each of them. I will only collect one sheet for each group. Use the other side for your answers.

A. The Cost-Benefit Principle and the Wonderful Invisible Hand

1. You are an energy-conservation-minded consumer whose only goal in choosing a car is to minimize the extent to which you deplete the planet's store of fossil fuels. You usually drive an average of 7,000 miles every year. If you can't afford to rent a new car, should you rent a 10-year-old Buick ($100/yr, 20 miles per gallon) or a 10-year-old Toyota ($300/yr, 40 mpg)? *To make things simple, assume the price of gasoline is $1/gallon.*

Buick: $100 + \frac{7000}{20} = \$450$

Toyota: $300 + \frac{7000}{40} = \$475$

I would get the toyota b/c for only $25 more and it conserves gas

* Buick b/c costs less and no one who drives more than you will choose the Buick. If you don't drive the Buick someone else will — if you drive Buick, less gas used overall.

61

B. People respond to Incentives – For next class

Try to use this idea of people *respond to incentives* to answer the following question.

2. Virginia Postrel, a columnist for the *New York Times*, has declared that income tax rates are a feminist issue, since they discourage women from participating in the labor force, hence increasing gender inequality. **Why does an increase in the tax rates discourage women from participating in the labor force?**
3. The other day I was at Burger King (not to eat though since I'm vegetarian) and notice the following sign next to the cash register: "Your meal is free if you failed to receive a receipt from the cashier. Please see the manager" **Why in the world Burger King want to give people anything for free only for failing to receive the receipt from the cashier?**
4. Johnson and Johnson (J &J), the giant pharmaceutical company, is running television ads promoting nursing as a rewarding career (they have even created a website). **Call me crazy, but I doubt J&J is doing this out of the good of their hearts; what do you think?**

B. People respond to Incentives – For next class

Try to use this idea of people *respond to incentives* to answer the following question.

2. Virginia Postrel, a columnist for the *New York Times*, has declared that income tax rates are a feminist issue, since they discourage women from participating in the labor force, hence increasing gender inequality. **Why does an increase in the tax rates discourage women from participating in the labor force?**
3. The other day I was at Burger King (not to eat though since I'm vegetarian) and notice the following sign next to the cash register: "Your meal is free if you failed to receive a receipt from the cashier. Please see the manager" **Why in the world Burger King want to give people anything for free only for failing to receive the receipt from the cashier?**
4. Johnson and Johnson (J &J), the giant pharmaceutical company, is running television ads promoting nursing as a rewarding career (they have even created a website). **Call me crazy, but I doubt J&J is doing this out of the good of their hearts; what do you think?**

ECON 02   Name: Kaitlyn Lagesse

Prof. Jose Vazquez-Cognet   TA: Yang Liu
LAB #

Our First Model: the Production Possibilities Frontier

I.   Study and Socializing

For a college student, the opportunity cost of time is usually in terms of two activities: studying versus socializing. Come on, be honest, this is probably one of the most difficult trade-offs you have to face every week. So, why not use that problem to introduce the first model you'll learn on this class: the **Production Possibilities Frontier.**
Suppose every week a student here on campus (maybe you?) has to make a decision between studying (essays to write) and socializing (people to meet). Specifically, each week, you have 40 hrs available, which you have to split among these two activities. Further, assume that this student needs *4 hrs to write 1 essay*, and, also, that he/she needs *2 hrs of socializing to meet 1 new person.*

1. Now, let's see if you can draw a diagram of your weekly production possibilities with the number of new people you meet every week on the horizontal axis (x-axis) and number of essays you write every week on the vertical essays (y-axis). In other words, on the y-axis identify the max number of essays you can write in 40 hrs if you use all your time for writing essays, and on the x-axis identify the maximum number of new people you can meet if you use all your time to meet people (socializing). In essence, this will be your *production possibilities* for a typical week.

Studying (# of essays/week)

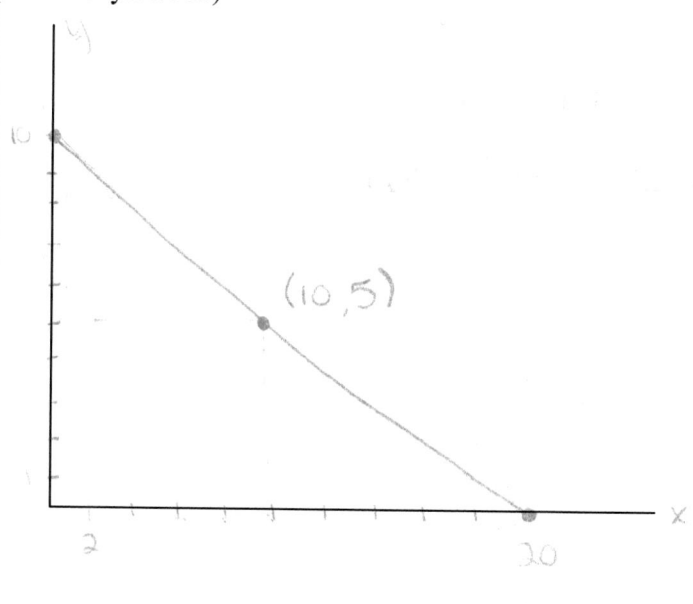

(10, 5)

Socializing (# of people met/week)

2. Good, now, answer this (for each case, answer using both math and the graph):
   a. Do you think you could write 6 essays and meet 8 new people in one week?

   Yes

   b. Do you think you could write 4 essays and meet 12 new people in one week?

   Yes

   c. Do you think you could write 8 essays and meet 6 new people in one week?

   No

   d. Do you think you could write 2 essays and meet 12 new people in one week?

   Yes

3. O.k. so now that you have your Production Possibilities Frontier (PPF), let see what is it good for.
   a. First, see if you can calculate the slope of this line (PPF).

   $m = \frac{-10}{20} = -\frac{1}{2}$

   i. Is the slope positive or negative?

   Negative

   b. Now, answer this: how many essays you won't be able to write for every new person you meet (hint: to answer this, think about how many essays you give up in order to meet 20 new people and then go from there)?

   $\frac{\text{new person}}{\text{essay}} = \frac{2}{4} = \frac{1}{2}$

   c. How many people you won't be able to meet for every new essay you write?

   $\frac{\text{essay}}{\text{person}} = \frac{4}{2} = 2$

   d. Look at the slope of your line (part a); do you see the opportunity costs you have calculated there? How come? Take a minute, think about it, talk about it with your lab partner, and try to explain why.

   e. Finally, suppose all of a sudden you took a writing course, which allows you to write essays a lot faster (at a rate of 1 every 2 hours):

   i. Draw a new PPF reflecting this change in technology.
   ii. What would happen to the cost of essays? decreases
   iii. What would happen to the cost of meeting new people? Increases

2. Good, now, answer this (for each case, answer using both math and the graph):
   a. Do you think you could write 6 essays and meet 8 new people in one week?

   Yes

   b. Do you think you could write 4 essays and meet 12 new people in one week?

   Yes

   c. Do you think you could write 8 essays and meet 6 new people in one week?

   No

   d. Do you think you could write 2 essays and meet 12 new people in one week?

   Yes

3. O.k. so now that you have your Production Possibilities Frontier (PPF), let see what is it good for.
   a. First, see if you can calculate the slope of this line (PPF).

   $m = \frac{-10}{20} = -\frac{1}{2}$ (-.5)

      i. Is the slope positive or negative?

      Negative

   b. Now, answer this: how many essays you won't be able to write for every new person you meet (hint: to answer this, think about how many essays you give up in order to meet 20 new people and then go from there)?

   $\frac{2}{4} = \frac{1}{2}$

   c. How many people you won't be able to meet for every new essay you write?

   $\frac{4}{2} = 2$

   d. Look at the slope of your line (part a); do you see the opportunity costs you have calculated there? How come? Take a minute, think about it, talk about it with your lab partner, and try to explain why.

   e. Finally, suppose all of a sudden you took a writing course, which allows you to write essays a lot faster (at a rate of 1 every 2 hours):

      i. Draw a new PPF reflecting this change in technology.
      ii. What would happen to the cost of essays? decreases
      iii. What would happen to the cost of meeting new people? increases

4. So, what did we learn? Take another few minutes and write the two most important things you learned about the PPF by using this example.

II. **Production Possibilities Frontier and National Security**

5. O.k., now lets do a more relevant example (and I'm not saying that the trade-offs of a college student are not important). One of the best uses of the PPF is to understand the difficult trade-offs the government has to make when it decides to allocate its resources. One of the most important of these trade-offs is the one between allocating resources for National Security (military) versus allocating resources towards solving the other social needs (food, shelter) of its citizens. Economists refer to this problem as: the guns vs. butter problem. A nation could either make more guns (National Security/Defense) or more butter (to feed the hungry).
   a. Use the following diagram to draw the PPF between butter and guns for a nation such as US. Remember, you can use any shape you want, but remember that you will have to defend your drawing when we you are done. For now the "actual" values are not important, just the shape. So, take your time and think about it first.

Other Resources (i.e. pounds of butter/year)

National Security (i.e. # of guns/ year)

4. So, what did we learn? Take another few minutes and write the two most important things you learned about the PPF by using this example.

II. **Production Possibilities Frontier and National Security**

5. O.k., now lets do a more relevant example (and I'm not saying that the trade-offs of a college student are not important). One of the best uses of the PPF is to understand the difficult trade-offs the government has to make when it decides to allocate its resources. One of the most important of these trade-offs is the one between allocating resources for National Security (military) versus allocating resources towards solving the other social needs (food, shelter) of its citizens. Economists refer to this problem as: the guns vs. butter problem. A nation could either make more guns (National Security/Defense) or more butter (to feed the hungry).
    a. Use the following diagram to draw the PPF between butter and guns for a nation such as US. Remember, you can use any shape you want, but remember that you will have to defend your drawing when we you are done. For now the "actual" values are not important, just the shape. So, take your time and think about it first.

Other Resources (i.e. pounds of butter/year)

National Security (i.e. # of guns/ year)

b. Now suppose the model you created in (a) was for the situation in US before the economic recession the U.S. is experiencing right now: how does the model looks now that we are in a recession? Draw two points in the diagram: 1) Before recession, and 2) after recession.

c. Do you think that the opportunity cost of a unit of national security has increased or decreased in the last five years?

b. Now suppose the model you created in (a) was for the situation in US before the economic recession the U.S. is experiencing right now: how does the model looks now that we are in a recession? Draw two points in the diagram: 1) Before recession, and 2) after recession.

c. Do you think that the opportunity cost of a unit of national security has increased or decreased in the last five years?

ECON 102   Name: Kaitlyn Lagesse

Prof. Jose Vazquez-Cognet   TA: Yang Liu, BQ3, F 10-10:50
LAB # 3

Our First Model: the Production Possibilities Frontier

I.   Study and Socializing

For a college student, the opportunity cost of time is usually in terms of two activities: studying versus socializing. Come on, be honest, this is probably one of the most difficult trade-offs you have to face every week. So, why not use that problem to introduce the first model you'll learn on this class: the **Production Possibilities Frontier.**

Suppose every week a student here on campus (maybe you?) has to make a decision between studying (essays to write) and socializing (people to meet). Specifically, each week, you have 40 hrs available, which you have to split among these two activities. Further, assume that this student needs *4 hrs to write 1 essay*, and, also, that he/she needs *2 hrs of socializing to meet 1 new person*.

1. Now, let's see if you can draw a diagram of your weekly production possibilities with the number of new people you meet every week on the horizontal axis (x-axis) and number of essays you write every week on the vertical essays (y-axis). In other words, on the y-axis identify the max number of essays you can write in 40 hrs if you use all your time for writing essays, and on the x-axis identify the maximum number of new people you can meet if you use all your time to meet people (socializing). In essence, this will be your *production possibilities* for a typical week.

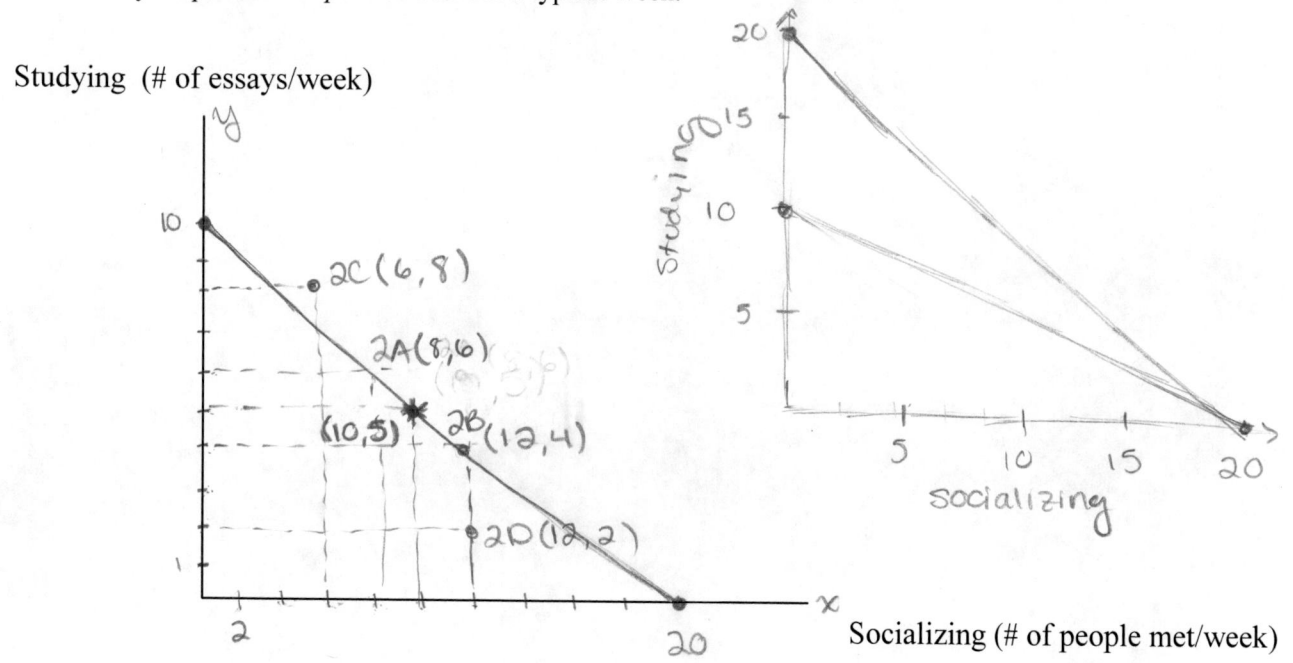

Studying (# of essays/week)

Socializing (# of people met/week)

cost of what you have x-axis = slope of line
cost of what you have y-axis = reciprocal of slope

P.C. of getting 20 #s is 10 essays
P.C. of getting 5 #s is 8 essays

$$\frac{20}{10} = \frac{5}{8}$$

$$\frac{80}{40} = \frac{25}{40}$$

$$\frac{16}{8} = \frac{5}{8} \rightarrow \frac{10}{8}$$

10 #s for 8 essays

4 hrs

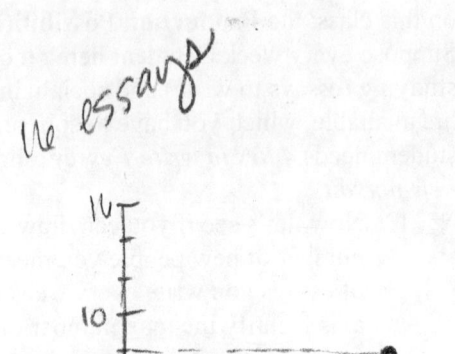

16 essays

16
10
2
   2   10

20 numbers

ECON 102

Prof. Jose Vazquez-Cognet

Name Kaitlyn Lagesse

TA Yang Liu, BQ3, F 10-10:50

Why do we trade? To write more essays and socialize more.

Study and Socializing

Last time we figured out how to model one of the most important trade-offs for a typical college student: studying versus socializing. Now let's use that example to answer the question: *is it possible to write more essays and socialize more if students traded with each other?* In order to conceptualize better the issue of trade, let's change the units of "socializing" from "new people" to "new phone numbers". So now every week a student here on campus (maybe you?) has to make a decision between studying (essays to write) and socializing (getting new phone numbers). Everything else stays the same: each week, you have 40 hrs available, which you have to split among these two activities. Also, you need 4 hrs to write 1 essay, and 2 hrs of socializing to get a new phone number. Finally, assume that a phone number traded is a phone number that can not be used.

1. Now, use the left side diagram below to draw your PPF if Trade is not allowed.

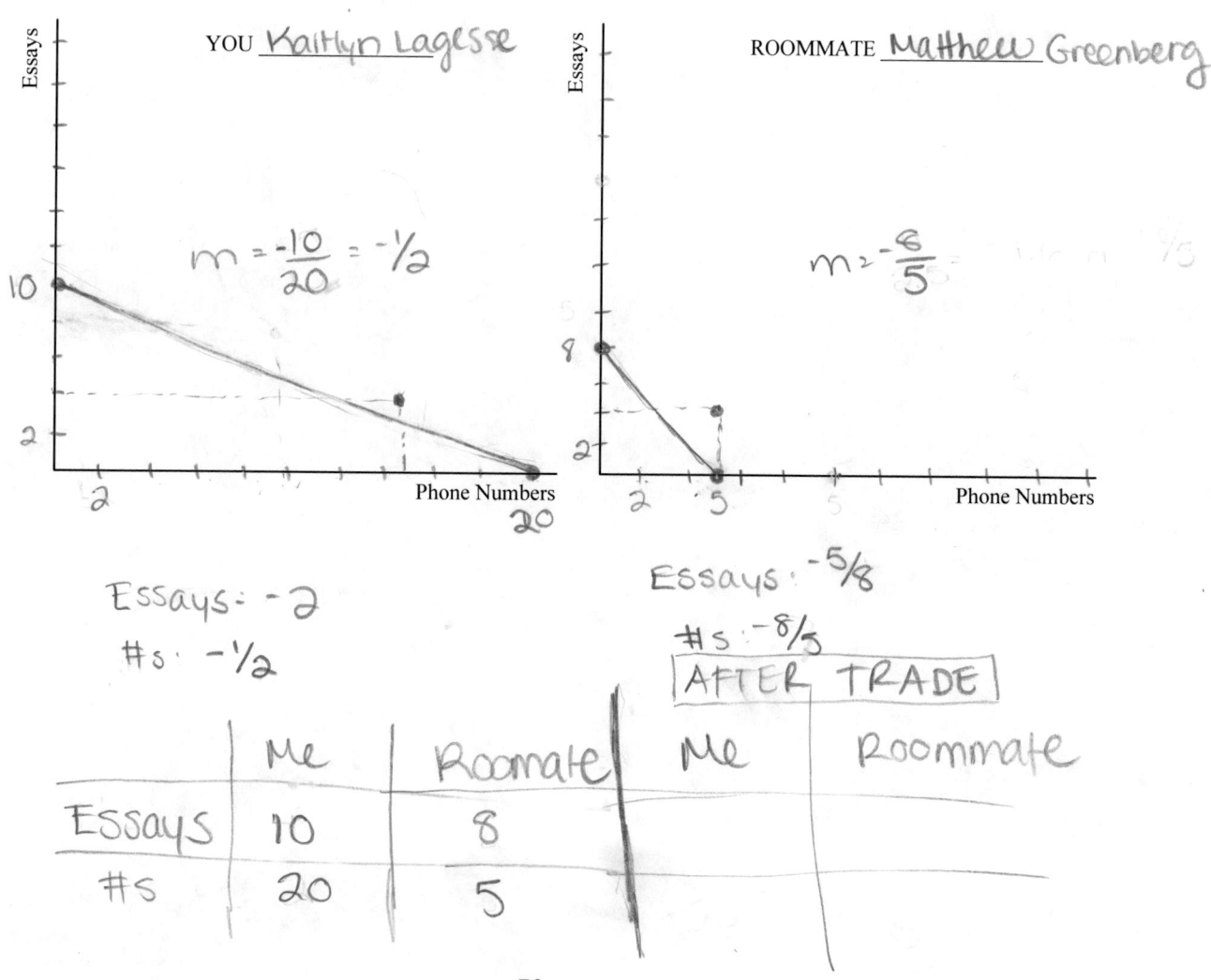

YOU Kaitlyn Lagesse

$m = \frac{-10}{20} = -\frac{1}{2}$

ROOMMATE Matthew Greenberg

$m = \frac{-8}{5}$

Essays: -2
#s: -1/2

Essays: -5/8
#s: -8/5

AFTER TRADE

	Me	Roomate	Me	Roommate
Essays	10	8		
#s	20	5		

73

ECON 102 Name: Kaitlyn Lagesse

Prof. Jose Vazquez-Cognet TA: Yang Liu, 13Q3, F 10-10:50

Why do we trade? To write more essays and socialize more.

Study and Socializing

Last time we figured out how to model one of the most important trade-offs for a typical college student: studying versus socializing. Now let's use that example to answer the question: *is it possible to write more essays and socialize more if students traded with each other?* In order to conceptualize better the issue of trade, let's change the units of "socializing" from "new people" to "new phone numbers". So now every week a student here on campus (maybe you?) has to make a decision between studying (essays to write) and socializing (getting new phone numbers). Everything else stays the same: each week, you have 40 hrs available, which you have to split among these two activities. Also, you need 4 hrs to write 1 essay, and 2 hrs of socializing to get a new phone number. Finally, assume that a phone number traded is a phone number that can not be used.

1. Now, use the left side diagram below to draw your PPF if Trade is not allowed.

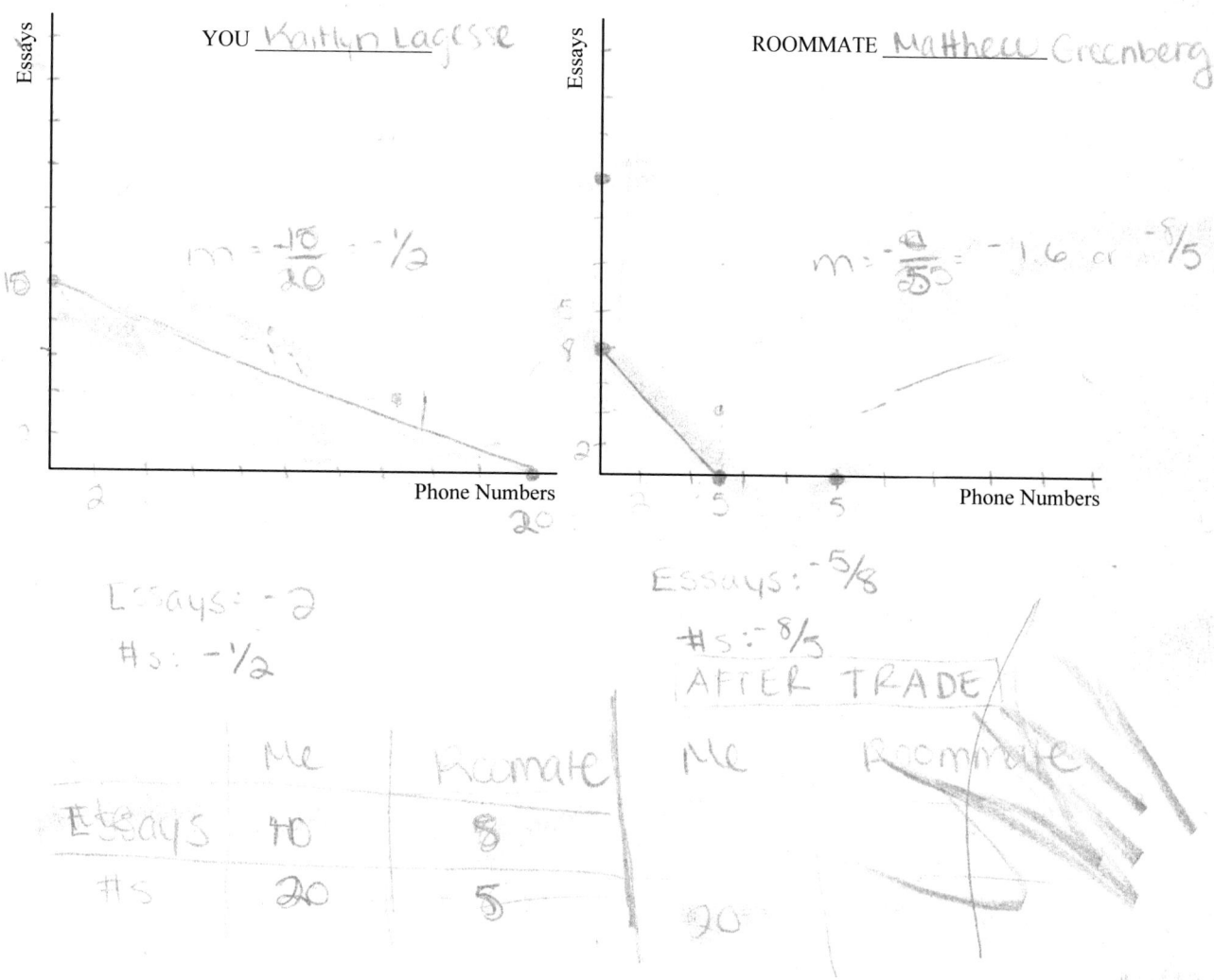

YOU: Kaitlyn Lagesse

ROOMMATE: Matthew Greenberg

$m = -\frac{10}{20} = -\frac{1}{2}$

$m = -\frac{8}{5} = -1.6$ or $-\frac{8}{5}$

Essays: −2
#s: −½

Essays: −5/8
#s: −8/5

AFTER TRADE

	Me	Roomate
Essays	10	8
#s	20	5

	Me	Roomate
	20	

73

2. Now, suppose you are considering sharing your tasks with your roommate. The problem is that your roommate is much worst at writing essays (it takes him/her 5 hrs to write an essay) and terrible at socializing (it takes her/him 8 hrs to get a new phone number). *Answer each of the following questions after completing all the necessary calculations. You may need to use the table below.*

   a) Do you think you would be better off by sharing these tasks with your roommate? Explain.

   Yes, you can both improve your PPF

   b) What would you do and what would you have your roommate do?

   I would do phone numbers and my roommate would write essays.

   c) What would be the terms of trade? (How many essays would be traded for each phone # and vice versa).

   Every 5 phone numbers would be worth four essays

   d) How many essays and how many phone numbers you would be able to "consume" if you traded with your roommate?

	ESSAY	PHONE #
Me	4	15
Roommate	4	5

   PRODUCTION | TRADE | CONSUMP.

	E	#	E	#	E	#
You	3	14	Get 3	Give 3	6	11
Room	8	0	Give 3	Get 3	5	3

	OPPRTUNITY COST OF EACH:	
	ESSAY	PHONE #
YOU	4/15 phone #s	15/4 essays
YOUR ROOMATE	4/5 phone #s	5/4 essays

   $m = \frac{4}{15}$ $m = \frac{4}{5}$

2. Now, suppose you are considering sharing your tasks with your roommate. The problem is that your roommate is much worst at writing essays (it takes him/her 5 hrs to write an essay) and terrible at socializing (it takes her/him 8 hrs to get a new phone number). *Answer each of the following questions after completing all the necessary calculations. You may need to use the table below.*

   a) Do you think you would be better off by sharing these tasks with your roommate? Explain.

   Yes you can both improve your PPF

   b) What would you do and what would you have your roommate do?

   I would do phone numbers and my roommate would write essays.

   c) What would be the terms of trade? (How many essays would be traded for each phone # and vice versa).

   Every 4 phone numbers would be worth four essays

   d) How many essays and how many phone numbers you would be able to "consume" if you traded with your roommate?

	ESSAY	PHONE #
Me	15	15
Roommate	5	5

	OPPRTUNITY COST OF EACH:	
	ESSAY	PHONE #
YOU	5 phone #s	4 essays
YOUR ROOMATE	5 phone #s	4 essays

$m = \frac{15}{15} = -3$ $m = \frac{5}{5}$

$\frac{5}{15} = -1/3$ $\frac{4}{5}$

ECON 102   Name:_____

Prof. Jose Vazquez-Cognet   TA:_____

Supply and Demand for Fighting Illini Basketball Tickets

In order to introduce the main ideas of supply and demand lets use the example of the market for Fighting Illini men's basketball tickets. At the end of this example (probably next week) we will be able to use the model to understand the arguments against and in favor of increasing the price of tickets, or reducing the penalties for scalping.

The Demand for Fighting Illini Tickets

Usually, information about the relationship between the price and quantity of a product is given in a table call "a demand schedule" (can you think of a reason for this name?). The information contained in this demand schedule could further be represented in a graph (the famous demand curve). Doing this on your own will go a long way to show you some of the tricks when dealing with demand curves. We'll start very easy and then we will complicate things a little more.

Table 1: Demand for Fighting Illini Basketball Tickets

Price of Seats ($/ Seat Section C)	Quantity Demanded (x 100)
$0	240
$150	180
$200	160
$250	140
$300	120
$350	100
$400	80
$600	0

1. *Deriving the Curve*: use the information presented in the table to draw the market demand for tickets on the space provided below.

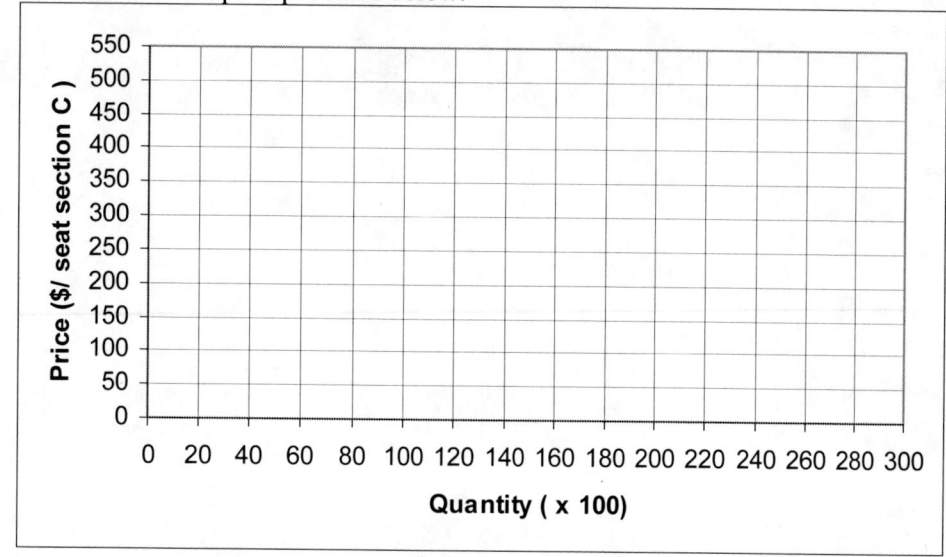

ECON 102   Name:_____

Prof. Jose Vazquez-Cognet   TA:_____

<u>**Supply and Demand for Fighting Illini Basketball Tickets**</u>

In order to introduce the main ideas of supply and demand lets use the example of the market for Fighting Illini men's basketball tickets. At the end of this example (probably next week) we will be able to use the model to understand the arguments against and in favor of increasing the price of tickets, or reducing the penalties for scalping.

The Demand for Fighting Illini Tickets

Usually, information about the relationship between the price and quantity of a product is given in a table call "a demand schedule" (can you think of a reason for this name?). The information contained in this demand schedule could further be represented in a graph (the famous demand curve). Doing this on your own will go a long way to show you some of the tricks when dealing with demand curves. We'll start very easy and then we will complicate things a little more.

Table 1: Demand for Fighting Illini Basketball Tickets

Price of Seats ($/ Seat Section C)	Quantity Demanded (x 100)
$0	240
$150	180
$200	160
$250	140
$300	120
$350	100
$400	80
$600	0

1. *Deriving the Curve*: use the information presented in the table to draw the market demand for tickets on the space provided below.

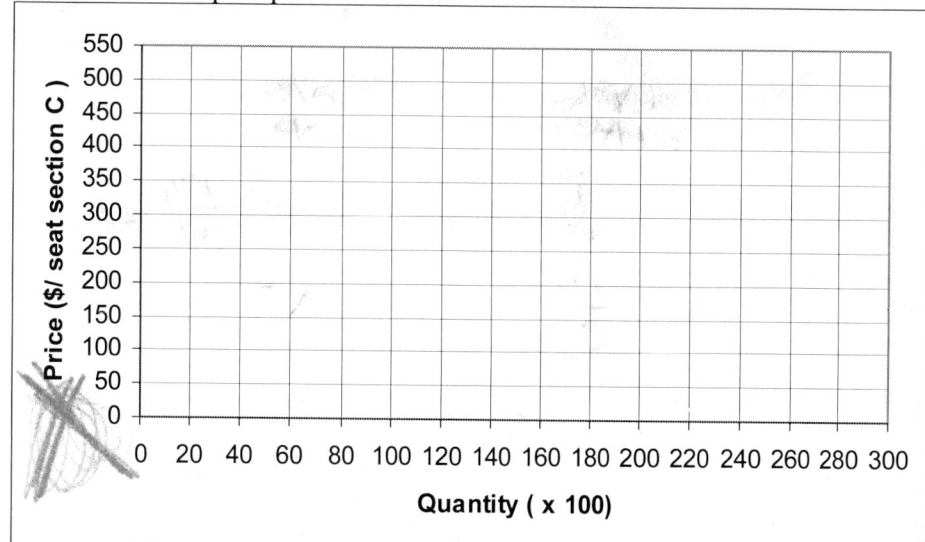

77

2. *Shifting the Curve*: use the diagram above to show the result of the following events in the market demand for tickets. On each case, just answer two questions: 1) would the curve shifts? and 2) which direction is the shift?

    a. The number of Fighting Illini basketball fans increases.

    b. The price of Fighting Illini **football** tickets is reduced (assume that football and basketball are substitutes).

    c. The income of Fighting Illini fans decreases.

    d. Fighting Illini basketball team looses 5 games in a row.

The Supply for Tickets

3. *Deriving the supply curve*: now lets do the supply. Since we've already computed demand, this should be a piece of cake. In order to understand the model better, we will assumed the supply is made of people wanting to sell tickets they buy from the university (scalpers).

Table 2: Supply for Fighting Illini Basketball Tickets

Price of Seats ($/ Seat Section C)	Quantity Supplied (x 100)
$100	0
$150	20
$200	40
$250	60
$300	80
$350	100
$400	120
$600	200

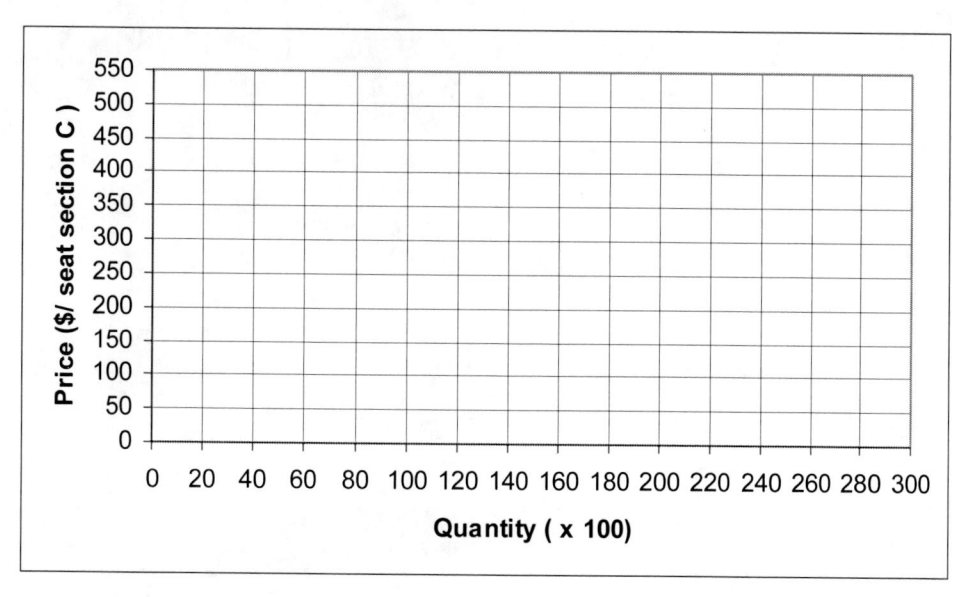

2. *Shifting the Curve*: use the diagram above to show the result of the following events in the market demand for tickets. On each case, just answer two questions: 1) would the curve shifts? and 2) which direction is the shift?

   a. The number of Fighting Illini basketball fans increases.

   b. The price of Fighting Illini **football** tickets is reduced (assume that football and basketball are substitutes).

   c. The income of Fighting Illini fans decreases.

   d. Fighting Illini basketball team looses 5 games in a row.

The Supply for Tickets

3. *Deriving the supply curve*: now lets do the supply. Since we've already computed demand, this should be a piece of cake. In order to understand the model better, we will assumed the supply is made of people wanting to sell tickets they buy from the university (scalpers).

Table 2: Supply for Fighting Illini Basketball Tickets

Price of Seats ($/ Seat Section C)	Quantity Supplied (x 100)
$100	0
$150	20
$200	40
$250	60
$300	80
$350	100
$400	120
$600	200

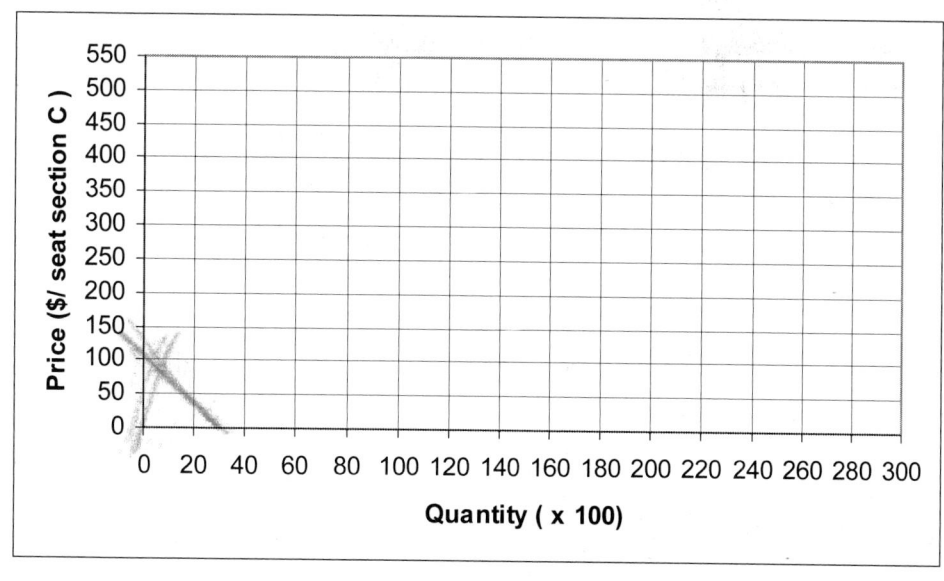

4. *Shifting the Curve*: use the diagram to show the result of the following events in the market supply for tickets. On each case, just answer two questions: 1) would the curve shifts? and 2) which direction is the shift?

   a. The number of scalpers suddenly increases.

   b. The cost of selling scalping tickets is suddenly reduced.

4. *Shifting the Curve*: use the diagram to show the result of the following events in the market supply for tickets. On each case, just answer two questions: 1) would the curve shifts? and 2) which direction is the shift?

   a. The number of scalpers suddenly increases.

   b. The cost of selling scalping tickets is suddenly reduced.

ECON 102   Name:_____

Prof. Jose Vazquez-Cognet   TA:_____

Supply and Demand for Fighting Illini Basketball Tickets

The Supply and Demand for Fighting Illini Basketball Tickets

1. *Using the model.* Now that we have a good idea of the market demand for tickets, we are in a good position to analyze how changes in the market will change the model. Show the effect of the following events on both the equilibrium price and quantity of tickets in the market. In each question, you must do the following: 1) shift the appropriate curve; 2) identify a new equilibrium point (label the new price P2 and the new quantity Q2). *On each case, assume ONLY ONE of the curves will shift; not both.*

    a. The university and the city government adopt a tough enforcement policy against scalping. Yet, tougher sentences are imposed **only on sellers** on scalping transactions.

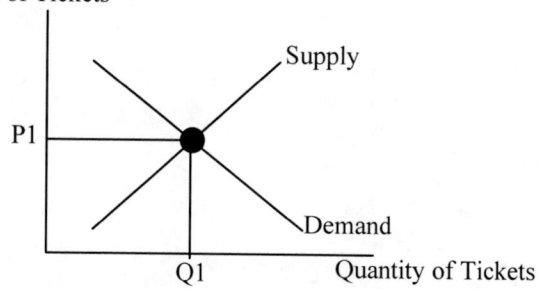

    b. Word is spread out that most of the best players are definitely not returning next year.

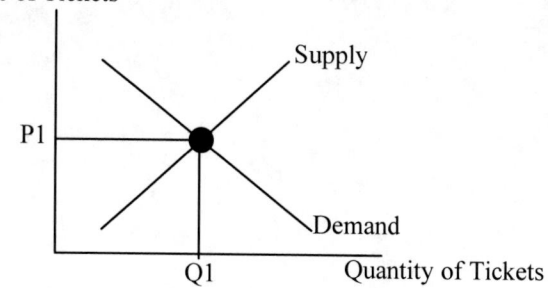

83

ECON 102   Name:_____

Prof. Jose Vazquez-Cognet   TA:_____

Supply and Demand for Fighting Illini Basketball Tickets

The Supply and Demand for Fighting Illini Basketball Tickets

1. *Using the model.* Now that we have a good idea of the market demand for tickets, we are in a good position to analyze how changes in the market will change the model. Show the effect of the following events on both the equilibrium price and quantity of tickets in the market. In each question, you must do the following: 1) shift the appropriate curve; 2) identify a new equilibrium point (label the new price P2 and the new quantity Q2). *On each case, assume ONLY ONE of the curves will shift; not both.*

    a. The university and the city government adopt a tough enforcement policy against scalping. Yet, tougher sentences are imposed **only on sellers** on scalping transactions.

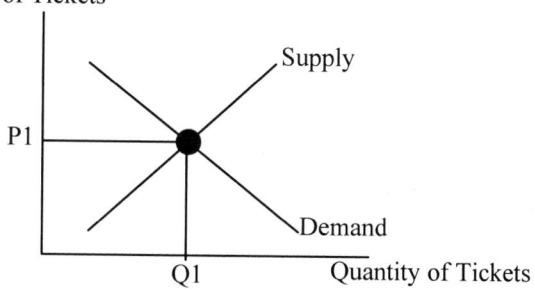

    b. Word is spread out that most of the best players are definitely not returning next year.

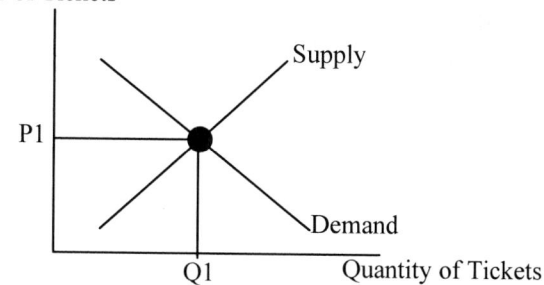

c. Scalping is legalized and in fact encourage by the city and the university.

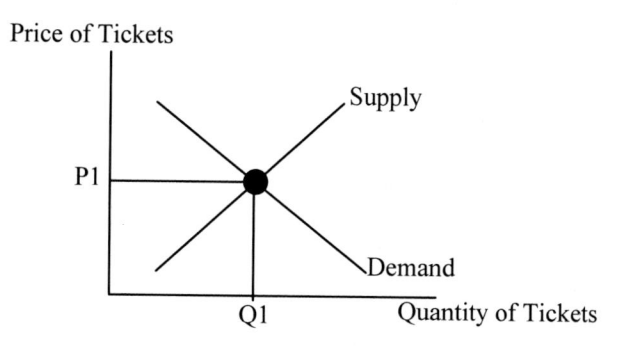

Price of Tickets

[Graph showing Supply and Demand curves intersecting at P1, Q1]

d. The football program is completely revamped and now the word spreads out the Fighting Illini will be strong contenders for the football title next year.

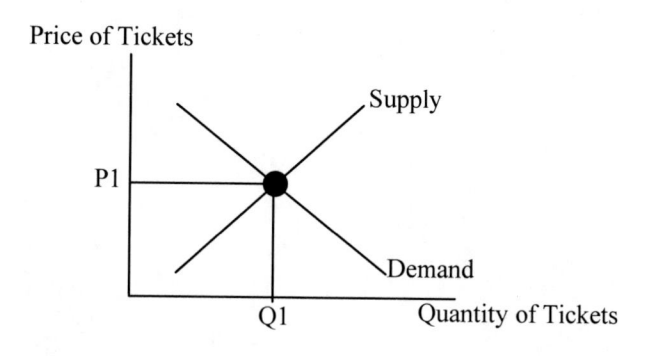

Price of Tickets

[Graph showing Supply and Demand curves intersecting at P1, Q1]

e. The university decides to increase its tuition.

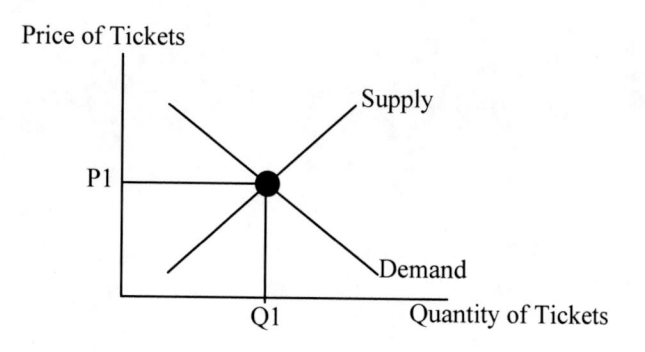

Price of Tickets

[Graph showing Supply and Demand curves intersecting at P1, Q1]

c. Scalping is legalized and in fact encourage by the city and the university.

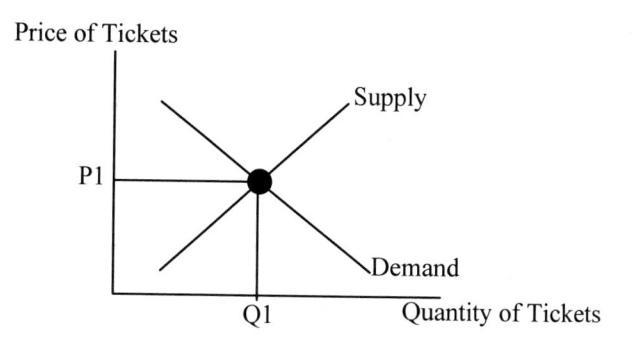

Price of Tickets vs *Quantity of Tickets* graph showing Supply and Demand curves intersecting at (Q1, P1).

d. The football program is completely revamped and now the word spreads out the Fighting Illini will be strong contenders for the football title next year.

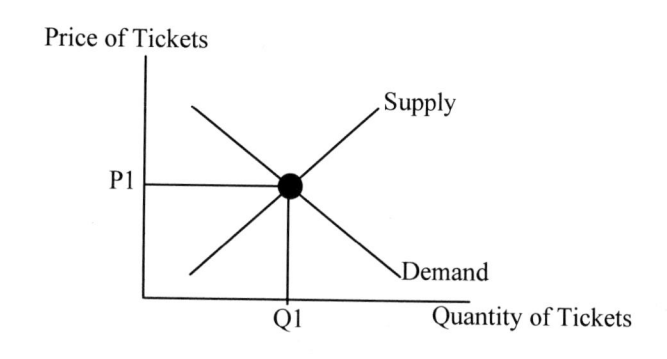

Price of Tickets vs *Quantity of Tickets* graph showing Supply and Demand curves intersecting at (Q1, P1).

e. The university decides to increase its tuition.

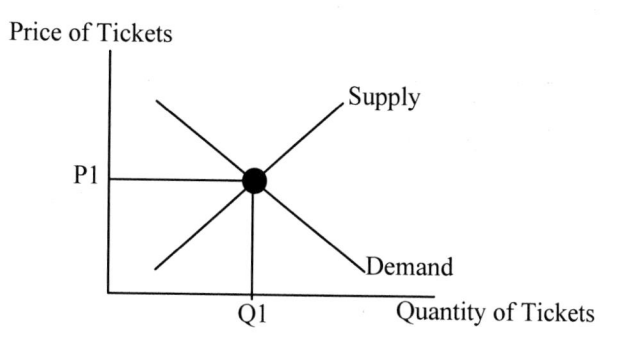

Price of Tickets vs *Quantity of Tickets* graph showing Supply and Demand curves intersecting at (Q1, P1).

ECON 102

Prof. Jose Vazquez-Cognet

Name:_____

TA:_____

Should Drug Use Be Legalized?

For many years economists have argued that the best way to deal with the crime related to the use of illegal drugs is simply to legalize them. In today's lecture we will explore the rationale for this argument.

The Effect of the War on Drugs

The diagram below shows a hypothetical market for cocaine in a particular city. Lets use this market to study the effects of two different government policies: a) a policy of strong enforcement that mainly targets the supply of drugs (a war against drugs), and b) a policy of strong public health intervention, that mainly targets the demand for cocaine (mainly addicts).

1. One of the main problems with the use of illegal drugs such as cocaine is the crime activity related to it. The level of this crime activity is arguably mostly related to the amount of money addicts have to spend buying the drugs, which, should be exactly the same as the revenue made by the suppliers. Economists call these two measures Total Expenditure and Total Revenue respectively. So let deal with that first.

    a. Calculate the Total Expenditure (TE) users of cocaine spend at the market equilibrium price and quantity (point A on the diagram).

    $$TE = Price \times Quantity = P \times Q = _____$$

    b. Now, suppose the government implements policy (a), mainly trying to reduce supply be enforcement. This is successful in reducing supply to a new equilibrium of P = $130 and Q = $90. Draw this change in the diagram and calculate the new TE cocaine addicts pay for the drugs (labeled the new equilibrium point B).

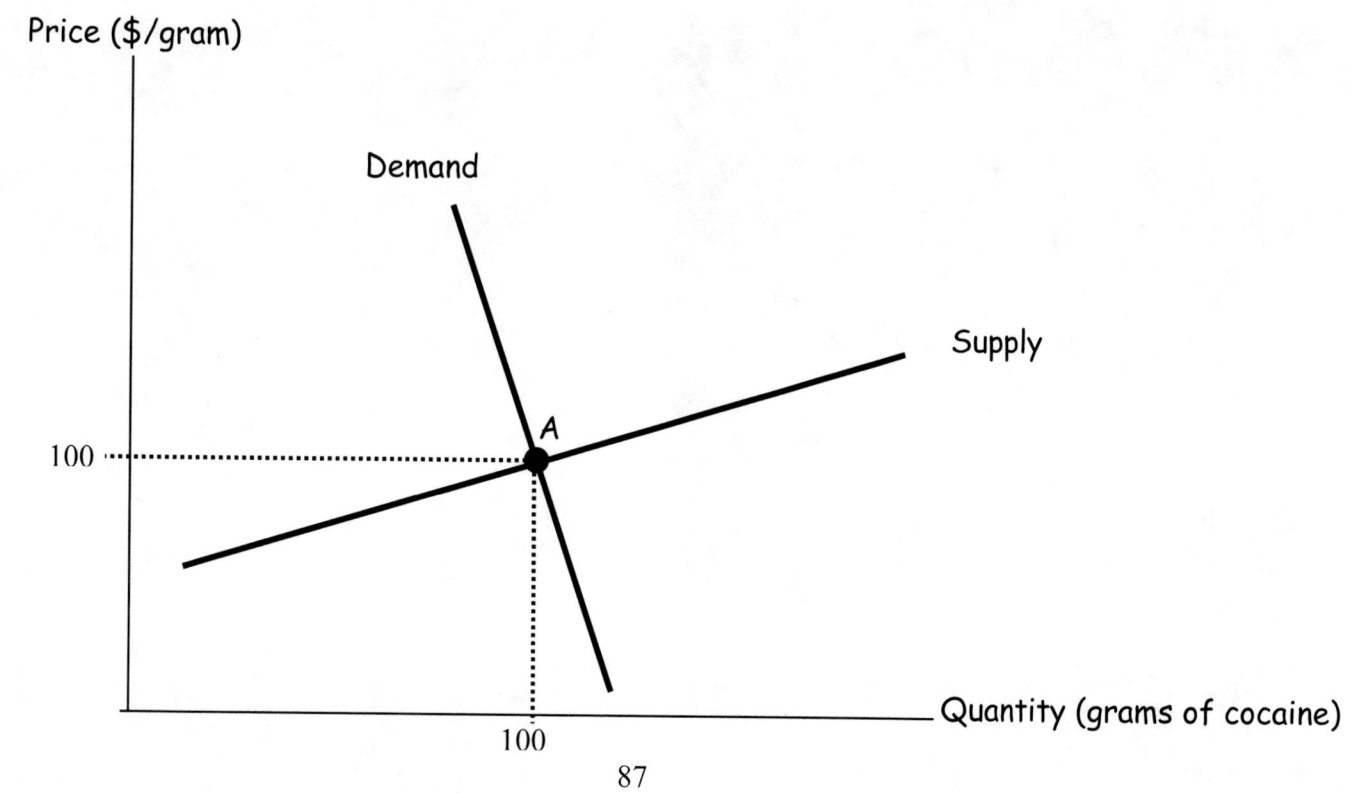

ECON 102   Name:_____

Prof. Jose Vazquez-Cognet   TA:_____

Should Drug Use Be Legalized?

For many years economists have argued that the best way to deal with the crime related to the use of illegal drugs is simply to legalize them. In today's lecture we will explore the rationale for this argument.

The Effect of the War on Drugs

The diagram below shows a hypothetical market for cocaine in a particular city. Lets use this market to study the effects of two different government policies: a) a policy of strong enforcement that mainly targets the supply of drugs (a war against drugs), and b) a policy of strong public health intervention, that mainly targets the demand for cocaine (mainly addicts).

1. One of the main problems with the use of illegal drugs such as cocaine is the crime activity related to it. The level of this crime activity is arguably mostly related to the amount of money addicts have to spend buying the drugs, which, should be exactly the same as the revenue made by the suppliers. Economists call these two measures Total Expenditure and Total Revenue respectively. So let deal with that first.

    a. Calculate the Total Expenditure (TE) users of cocaine spend at the market equilibrium price and quantity (point A on the diagram).

        TE = Price x Quantity = P x Q = _____

    b. Now, suppose the government implements policy (a), mainly trying to reduce supply be enforcement. This is successful in reducing supply to a new equilibrium of P = $130 and Q = $90. Draw this change in the diagram and calculate the new TE cocaine addicts pay for the drugs (labeled the new equilibrium point B).

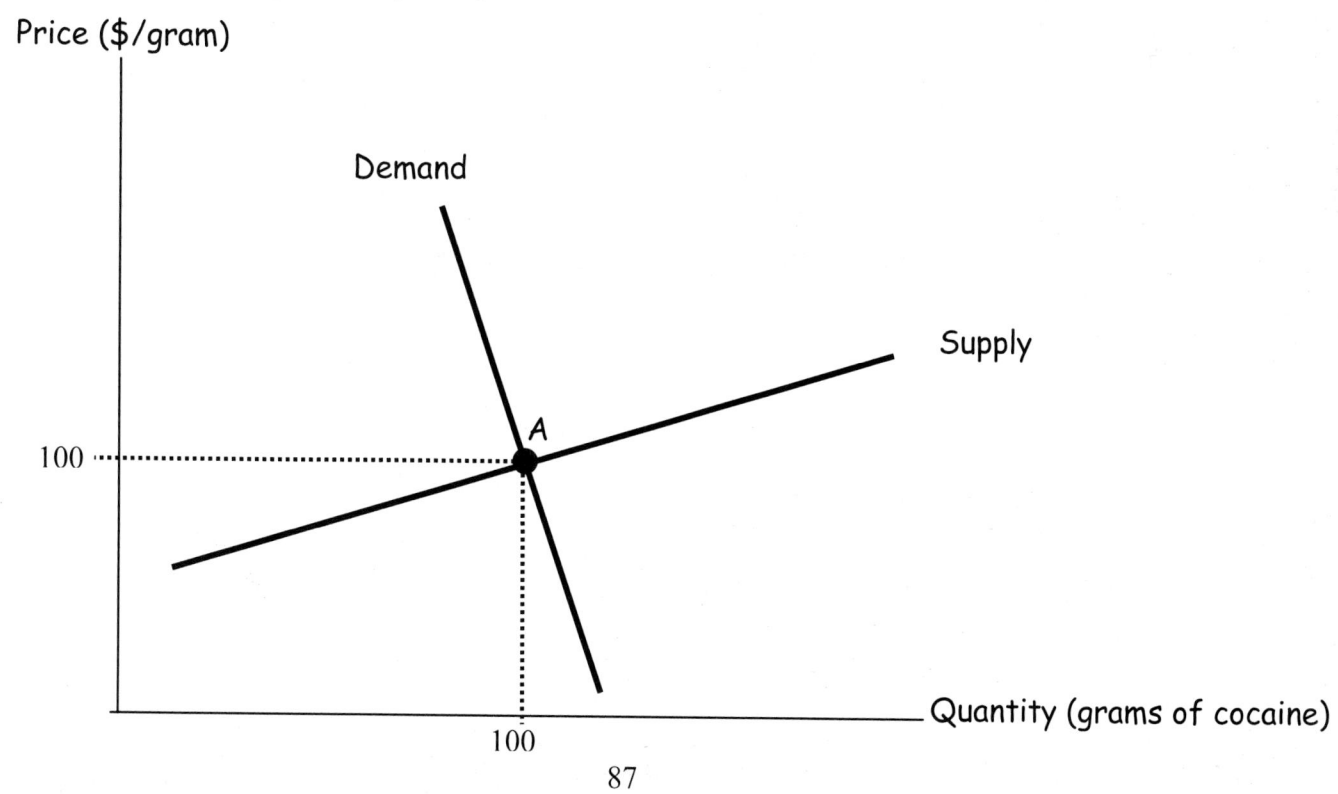

Price ($/gram)

[Graph showing Demand curve (steep, downward sloping) and Supply curve (upward sloping) intersecting at point A where Price = 100 and Quantity = 100]

Quantity (grams of cocaine)

c. Now suppose the government implements the second policy option, mainly trying to reduce demand. On this it is successful on reducing the demand enough to reach a new equilibrium of P = $90 and Q = 80. Draw this change on the diagram and calculate the new TE (labeled the new equilibrium point C).

d. Which one of the two measures would be more effective at reducing crime, (a) or (b). Explain why.

e. Now, what do you think would happen if the government legalized cocaine? Use the diagram below to answer this question. To answer, shifts the appropriate curve(s) and identify new equilibriums. Also, discuss what would happen to crime as a result.

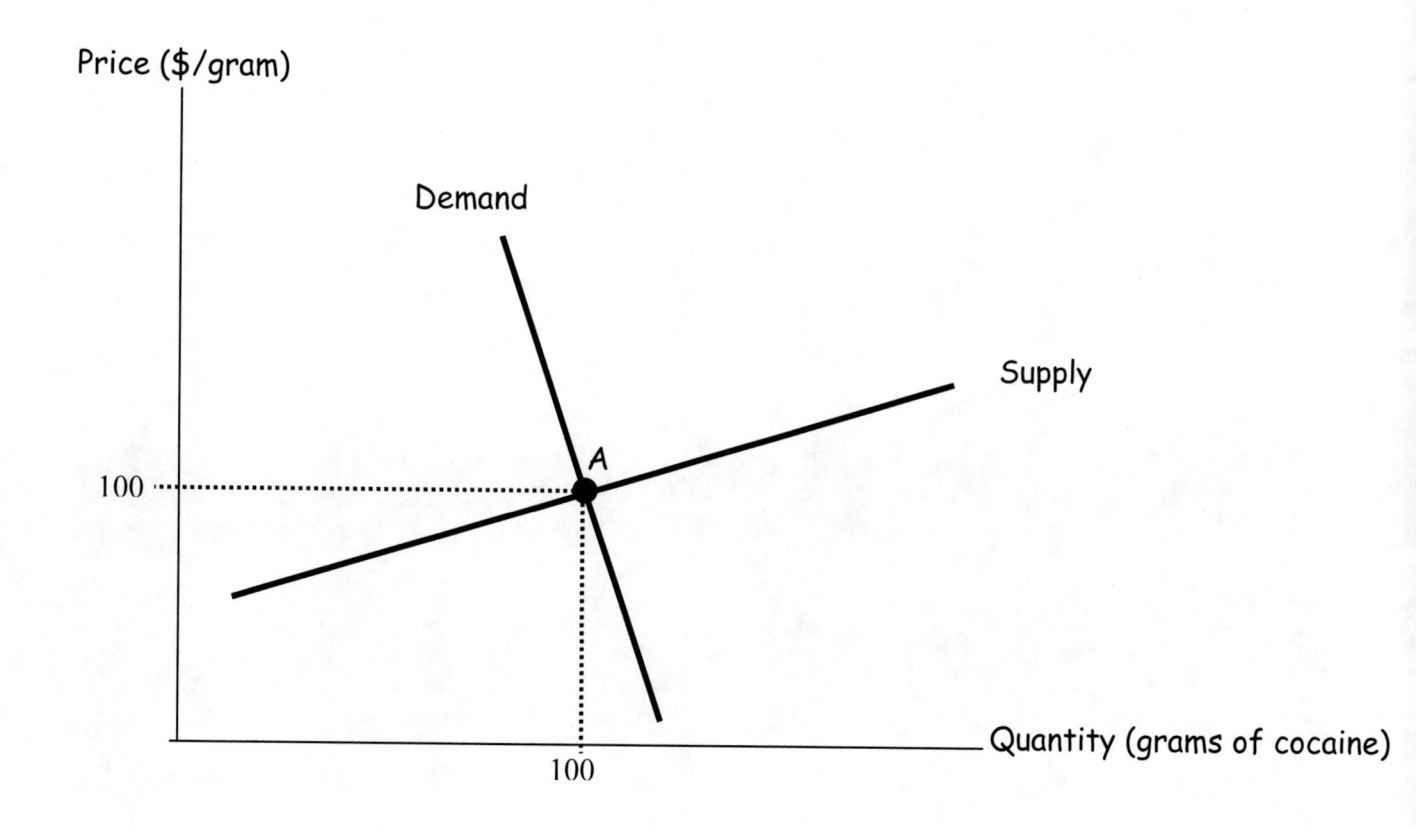

c. Now suppose the government implements the second policy option, mainly trying to reduce demand. On this it is successful on reducing the demand enough to reach a new equilibrium of P = $90 and Q = 80. Draw this change on the diagram and calculate the new TE (labeled the new equilibrium point C).

d. Which one of the two measures would be more effective at reducing crime, (a) or (b). Explain why.

e. Now, what do you think would happen if the government legalized cocaine? Use the diagram below to answer this question. To answer, shifts the appropriate curve(s) and identify new equilibriums. Also, discuss what would happen to crime as a result.

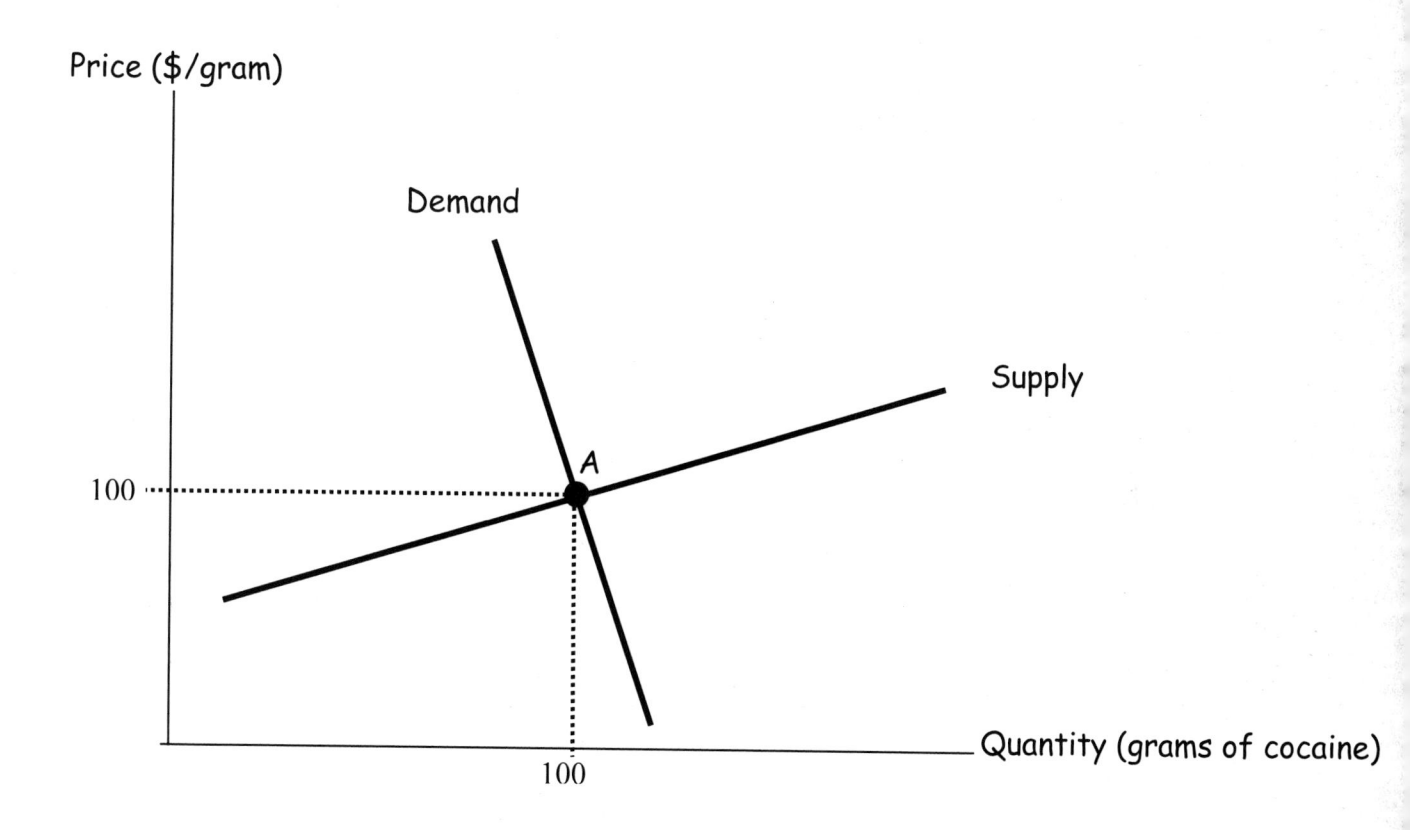

Now Lets Calculate the Elasticity

2. Calculate the price elasticity of demand between point A and point B on the first diagram above.

   a. Is the price elasticity of demand from A to B elastic, inelastic or unitary?

3. Calculate the price elasticity of supply between point A and C on the diagram below.

   a. Is the price elasticity of supply from A to C elastic, inelastic, or unitary?

Now Lets Calculate the Elasticity

2. Calculate the price elasticity of demand between point A and point B on the first diagram above.

   a. Is the price elasticity of demand from A to B elastic, inelastic or unitary?

3. Calculate the price elasticity of supply between point A and C on the diagram below.

   a. Is the price elasticity of supply from A to C elastic, inelastic, or unitary?

ECON 102

Prof. Jose Vazquez-Cognet

Name:_____

TA:_____

Should Drug Use Be Legalized? (A More Formal Approach)

Supply and Demand

1. Suppose demand for cocaine in the US is $Q_D = 400 - .28P$, while supply is given by $Q_S = -250 + 5P$:
    a. What would be the equilibrium price, P^*, and quantity, Q^*, on this market?

    b. Now suppose that through enforcement the government is successful in decreasing the supply of cocaine to $Q_S = -500 + 5P$. What would be the new equilibrium price and quantity in the market for cocaine?

    c. Do you think crime related to illegal drug trafficking will increase or decrease as a result of the decrease in supply? Answer given the change in total expenditures on cocaine before and after the change.

ECON 102

Name:_____

Prof. Jose Vazquez-Cognet

TA:_____

Should Drug Use Be Legalized? (A More Formal Approach)

Supply and Demand

1. Suppose demand for cocaine in the US is $Q_D = 400 - .28P$, while supply is given by $Q_S = -250 + 5P$:
    a. What would be the equilibrium price, P^*, and quantity, Q^*, on this market?

    b. Now suppose that through enforcement the government is successful in decreasing the supply of cocaine to $Q_S = -500 + 5P$. What would be the new equilibrium price and quantity in the market for cocaine?

    c. Do you think crime related to illegal drug trafficking will increase or decrease as a result of the decrease in supply? Answer given the change in total expenditures on cocaine before and after the change.

Elasticity

2. What would be the price elasticity of demand when the price is at the original equilibrium? (part a)

   a. What would be the price, when $\varepsilon = 1$?

More Problems
1. Assume the market demand for wheat may be written as
$$Q_D = 10{,}816 - 2{,}228P_R + 1251P_C + 6.28I$$

   where Q_D = quantity of roses sold (dozens); P_R = average wholesale price of roses ($/dozen); P_C = average wholesale price of carnations ($/dozen); and I average weekly family income ($/week).

   a. What happens to the Demand for Roses if the price for Carnations, P_R, goes up?
   b. What happens to the Demand for Roses if weekly income goes up?
   c. Assuming that currently you sell both roses and carnations at $1/dozen, and income is $20/week, calculate the price elasticity, and income elasticity for roses.

2. The price elasticity of demand for gasoline is estimated to be –0.2. Two million gallons are sold daily at a price of $1. Use this information to calculate a demand curve for gasoline assuming it is linear.

3. The elasticity of demand for tomatoes is .25. Because of ideal weather conditions, the farmers are anticipating a bumper crop of tomatoes. That is, the tomato harvest will be larger than average. Are they happy or sad about the prospects of a bumper crop?

Elasticity

2. What would be the price elasticity of demand when the price is at the original equilibrium? (part a)

   a. What would be the price, when $\varepsilon = 1$?

More Problems

1. Assume the market demand for wheat may be written as
$$Q_D = 10{,}816 - 2{,}228 P_R + 1251 P_C + 6.28 I$$

   where Q_D = quantity of roses sold (dozens); P_R = average wholesale price of roses ($/dozen); P_C = average wholesale price of carnations ($/dozen); and I average weekly family income ($/week).

   a. What happens to the Demand for Roses if the price for Carnations, P_R, goes up?
   b. What happens to the Demand for Roses if weekly income goes up?
   c. Assuming that currently you sell both roses and carnations at $1/dozen, and income is $20/week, calculate the price elasticity, and income elasticity for roses.

2. The price elasticity of demand for gasoline is estimated to be –0.2. Two million gallons are sold daily at a price of $1. Use this information to calculate a demand curve for gasoline assuming it is linear.

3. The elasticity of demand for tomatoes is .25. Because of ideal weather conditions, the farmers are anticipating a bumper crop of tomatoes. That is, the tomato harvest will be larger than average. Are they happy or sad about the prospects of a bumper crop?

3. Suppose the demand curve for garbanzo beans is given by

$$Q = 20 - P$$

where Q is thousands of pounds of beans bought per week and P is the price in dollars per pound

   a. How many beans will be bought at $P = 0$?

   b. At what price does the quantity demanded of beans become zero?

   c. Calculate total expenditures (P x Q) for beans of each whole dollar price between the prices identified in part a and part b.

   d. What price for beans yields the highest total expenditures?

   e. Suppose the demand for bean shifted to $Q = 40 - 2P$. How would your answers to part a through part d change? Explain the differences intuitively and with a graph

4. Explain why demand curves that are linear (straight lines) generally do not have a constant elasticity. What types of linear demand curves do have a constant elasticity?

3. Suppose the demand curve for garbanzo beans is given by

$$Q = 20 - P$$

where Q is thousands of pounds of beans bought per week and P is the price in dollars per pound

   a. How many beans will be bought at $P = 0$?

   b. At what price does the quantity demanded of beans become zero?

   c. Calculate total expenditures (P x Q) for beans of each whole dollar price between the prices identified in part a and part b.

   d. What price for beans yields the highest total expenditures?

   e. Suppose the demand for bean shifted to $Q = 40 - 2P$. How would your answers to part a through part d change? Explain the differences intuitively and with a graph

4. Explain why demand curves that are linear (straight lines) generally do not have a constant elasticity. What types of linear demand curves do have a constant elasticity?

ECON 102   Name:_____

Prof. Jose Vazquez-Cognet   TA:_____

How Uncle Sam Could Ease the Organ Shortage?

Today we are going to discuss a rather controversial, yet not much debated issue: the current system of organ donation in the US. To introduce this topic, let's see what a leading economist had to say on the subject:

> "It is essential to find ways to raise the supply of organs and ease the suffering and long wait that many sick persons now endure. That delay can cost lives: Almost 70 persons die each month while waiting for livers to become available."

Gary S. Becker. Business Week. New York: Jan 20, 1997.

Video/Movie Analysis

1. How do you feel about the illegal market for organ describe in the movie? Is it unfair to organ donors? Is it unfair to people who need to organs? Who benefits and who looses?

2. What do you think will be happen to the organ donors in the underground market (such as the people from the movie) for organs if a successful policy closes the organ shortage by increasing the rate of legal donations?

ECON 102   Name:_____

Prof. Jose Vazquez-Cognet   TA:_____

How Uncle Sam Could Ease the Organ Shortage?

Today we are going to discuss a rather controversial, yet not much debated issue: the current system of organ donation in the US. To introduce this topic, let's see what a leading economist had to say on the subject:

> "It is essential to find ways to raise the supply of organs and ease the suffering and long wait that many sick persons now endure. That delay can cost lives: Almost 70 persons die each month while waiting for livers to become available."

Gary S. Becker. Business Week. New York: Jan 20, 1997.

Video/Movie Analysis

1. How do you feel about the illegal market for organ describe in the movie? Is it unfair to organ donors? Is it unfair to people who need to organs? Who benefits and who looses?

2. What do you think will be happen to the organ donors in the underground market (such as the people from the movie) for organs if a successful policy closes the organ shortage by increasing the rate of legal donations?

ECON 102   Name:_____

Prof. Jose Vazquez-Cognet   TA:_____
LAB # 10

How Uncle Sam Could Ease the Organ Shortage (Part II)?

The Market for Organs

In 1984, Congress passed the National Organ Transplant Act to prohibit the sale and purchase of transplant organs in interstate commerce. Nevertheless, each year about 8,000 kidneys, 20,000 corneas, and 2,200 hearts are transplanted in the US.

1. Use the information above to draw a diagram for the market for kidneys in the US. Assume both curves are linear. The numbers are not important, just the shape/position of the curves (for instance, consider the fact that people will donate kidneys even when the price for a kidney is zero!)

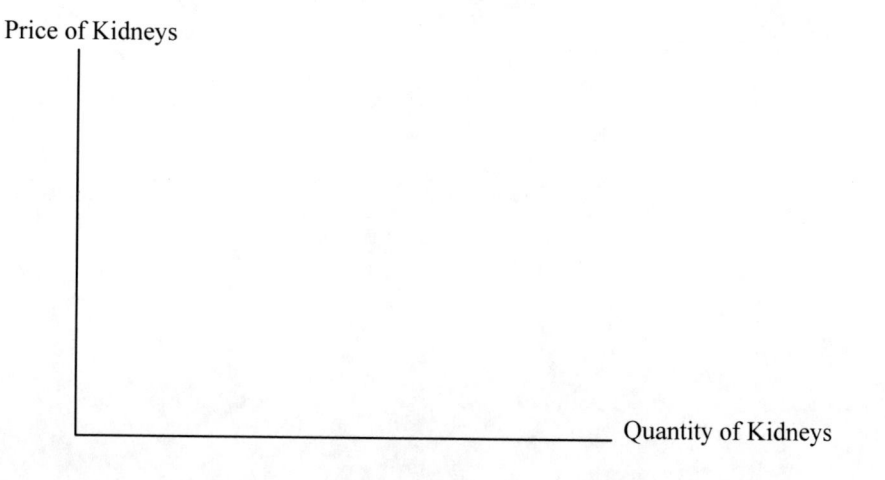

Price of Kidneys

Quantity of Kidneys

2. Now identify the consumer and producer surplus in your diagram, assuming kidneys were allowed to be sold freely in the market (there was no Ban prohibiting the sale of organs).

3. Now introduce the ban on selling kidneys into your model. How does this fact change your diagram of the market for organs in the US? Show the change in your diagram and write the explanation below.

ECON 102

Prof. Jose Vazquez-Cognet
LAB # 10

Name:_____

TA:_____

How Uncle Sam Could Ease the Organ Shortage (Part II)?

The Market for Organs
In 1984, Congress passed the National Organ Transplant Act to prohibit the sale and purchase of transplant organs in interstate commerce. Nevertheless, each year about 8,000 kidneys, 20,000 corneas, and 2,200 hearts are transplanted in the US.

1. Use the information above to draw a diagram for the market for kidneys in the US. Assume both curves are linear. The numbers are not important, just the shape/position of the curves (for instance, consider the fact that people will donate kidneys even when the price for a kidney is zero!)

Price of Kidneys

Quantity of Kidneys

2. Now identify the consumer and producer surplus in your diagram, assuming kidneys were allowed to be sold freely in the market (there was no Ban prohibiting the sale of organs).

3. Now introduce the ban on selling kidneys into your model. How does this fact change your diagram of the market for organs in the US? Show the change in your diagram and write the explanation below.

4. What is the efficiency effect of the National Organ Transplant Act? Use your diagram to identify the loss or gain of economic surplus as a result of this law (this is the deadweight loss).

5. Now think about the ways the government can meet the goals of the Act without the loss in economic welfare. Write a few sentences about the type of solutions to the problem.

4. What is the efficiency effect of the National Organ Transplant Act? Use your diagram to identify the loss or gain of economic surplus as a result of this law (this is the deadweight loss).

5. Now think about the ways the government can meet the goals of the Act without the loss in economic welfare. Write a few sentences about the type of solutions to the problem.

ECON 102   Name:_____

Prof. Jose Vazquez-Cognet   TA:_____

Who Should Pay for the Gas tax?

Today's lab should be completed in teams of three. We are going to study the best way to reduce gas consumption through taxes. For this, each person of your team will take one of the following three roles:

1. A lobbyist for business a group trying to mold policy in the advantage of cars manufacturers and other business dependent on consumption of gasoline.
2. A lobbyist for an environmental group (i.e. The Sierra Club) trying to mold policy in the advantage of protecting the environment.
3. A representative of the US Environmental Protection Agency (EPA). Your goal is to protect the environment and also to protect business (so in a way, you have the most challenging task of the three.)

At the same time, each member plays the role of consumers, since all of us will be affected by the tax.

The government is considering implementing one of two tax options:
        a) A tax on gasoline paid by sellers when the SELL the gasoline to consumers.
        b) A tax on gas-guzzling cars (i.e. SUVs) paid by manufactures when they make the cars.

Use the two diagrams on the next page, which describe the market conditions in this country on the relevant markets, to answer the following two questions:

1) Which of the two taxes is better for the group you are representing?
2) If you had in mind the welfare of the entire society, which tax do you proposed is better?

In answering these questions, each person should do the following:

- Use the diagram to show the impact of the tax on each of the different sectors of the population you are representing.
- Try to convince the others that your view is the best.

Finally, the government representative should choose a tax option based on the discussion. Consensus is not necessary, after all the government have the final vote. Write here your choice and how that will take with the two representatives.

_____

_____

_____

ECON 102   Name:_____

Prof. Jose Vazquez-Cognet   TA:_____

Who Should Pay for the Gas tax?

Today's lab should be completed in teams of three. We are going to study the best way to reduce gas consumption through taxes. For this, each person of your team will take one of the following three roles:

1. A lobbyist for business a group trying to mold policy in the advantage of cars manufacturers and other business dependent on consumption of gasoline.
2. A lobbyist for an environmental group (i.e. The Sierra Club) trying to mold policy in the advantage of protecting the environment.
3. A representative of the US Environmental Protection Agency (EPA). Your goal is to protect the environment and also to protect business (so in a way, you have the most challenging task of the three.)

At the same time, each member plays the role of consumers, since all of us will be affected by the tax.

The government is considering implementing one of two tax options:
   a) A tax on gasoline paid by sellers when the SELL the gasoline to consumers.
   b) A tax on gas-guzzling cars (i.e. SUVs) paid by manufactures when they make the cars.

Use the two diagrams on the next page, which describe the market conditions in this country on the relevant markets, to answer the following two questions:

1) Which of the two taxes is better for the group you are representing?
2) If you had in mind the welfare of the entire society, which tax do you proposed is better?

In answering these questions, each person should do the following:

- Use the diagram to show the impact of the tax on each of the different sectors of the population you are representing.
- Try to convince the others that your view is the best.

Finally, the government representative should choose a tax option based on the discussion. Consensus is not necessary, after all the government have the final vote. Write here your choice and how that will take with the two representatives.

_____

_____

_____

A Tax on Gasoline Sellers

Gasoline Market

Price / Quantity; S with tax, S without tax, D

Gas-guzzling cars Market

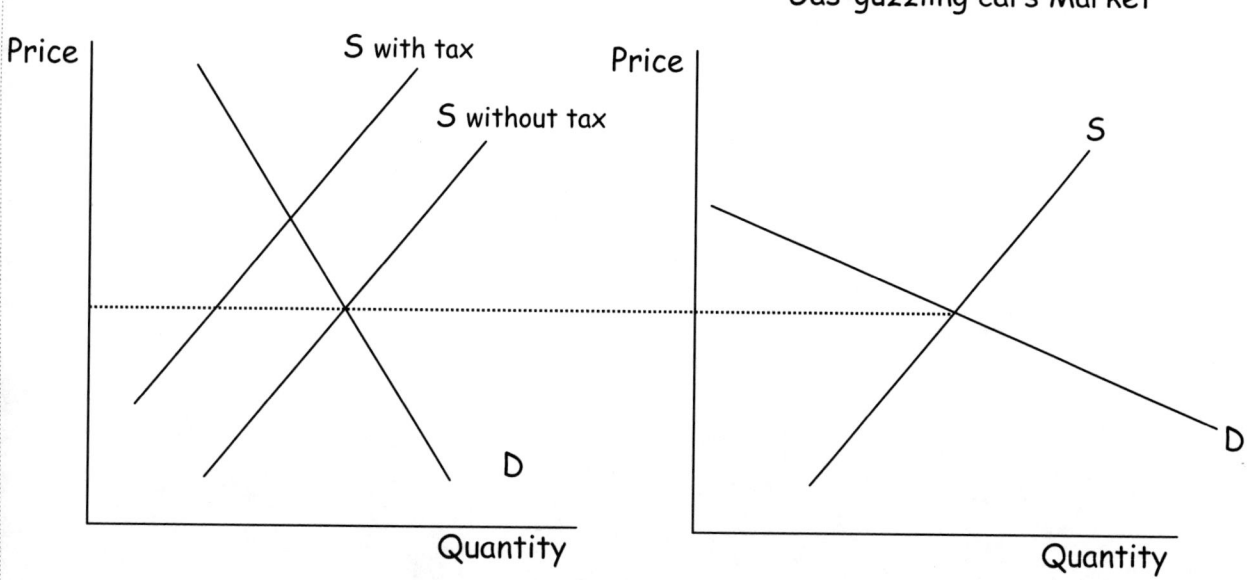

Price / Quantity; S, D

A Tax on Gas-guzzling cars Producers

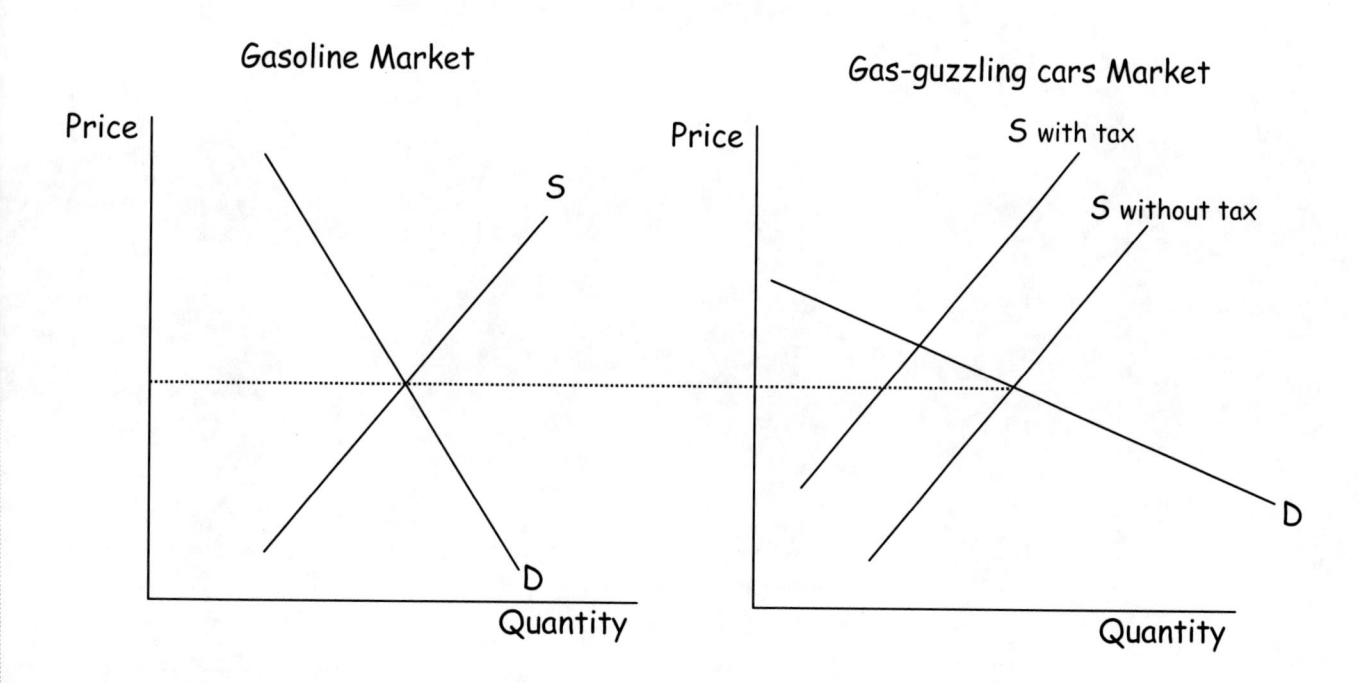

Gasoline Market

Price / Quantity; S, D

Gas-guzzling cars Market

Price / Quantity; S with tax, S without tax, D

A Tax on Gasoline Sellers

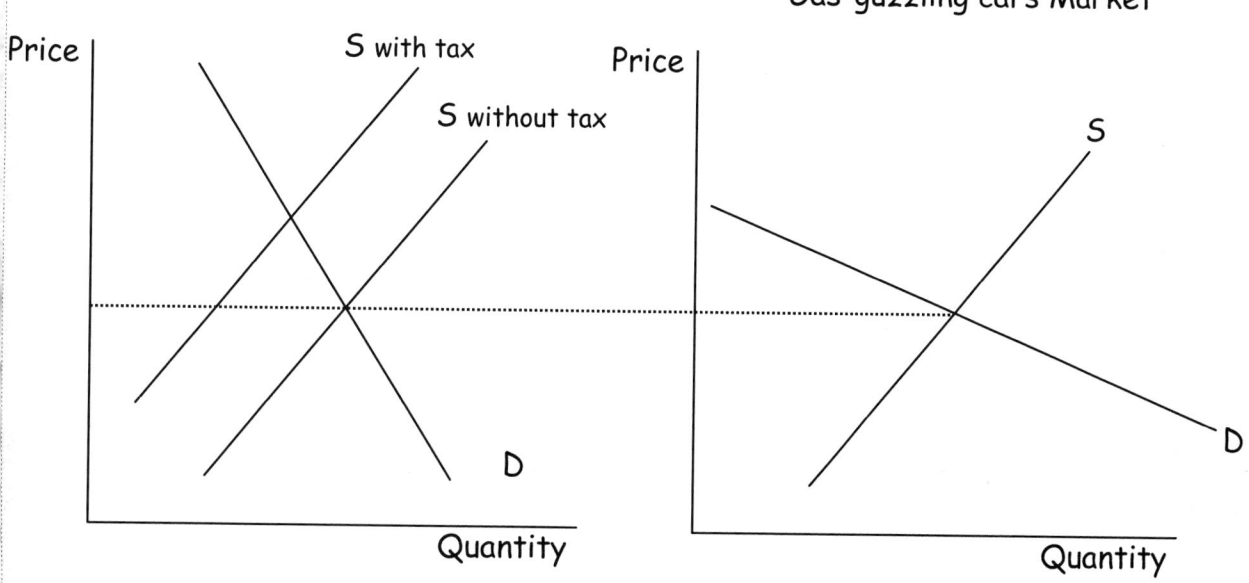

Gasoline Market

Price / Quantity
S with tax, S without tax, D

Gas-guzzling cars Market

Price / Quantity
S, D

A Tax on Gas-guzzling cars Producers

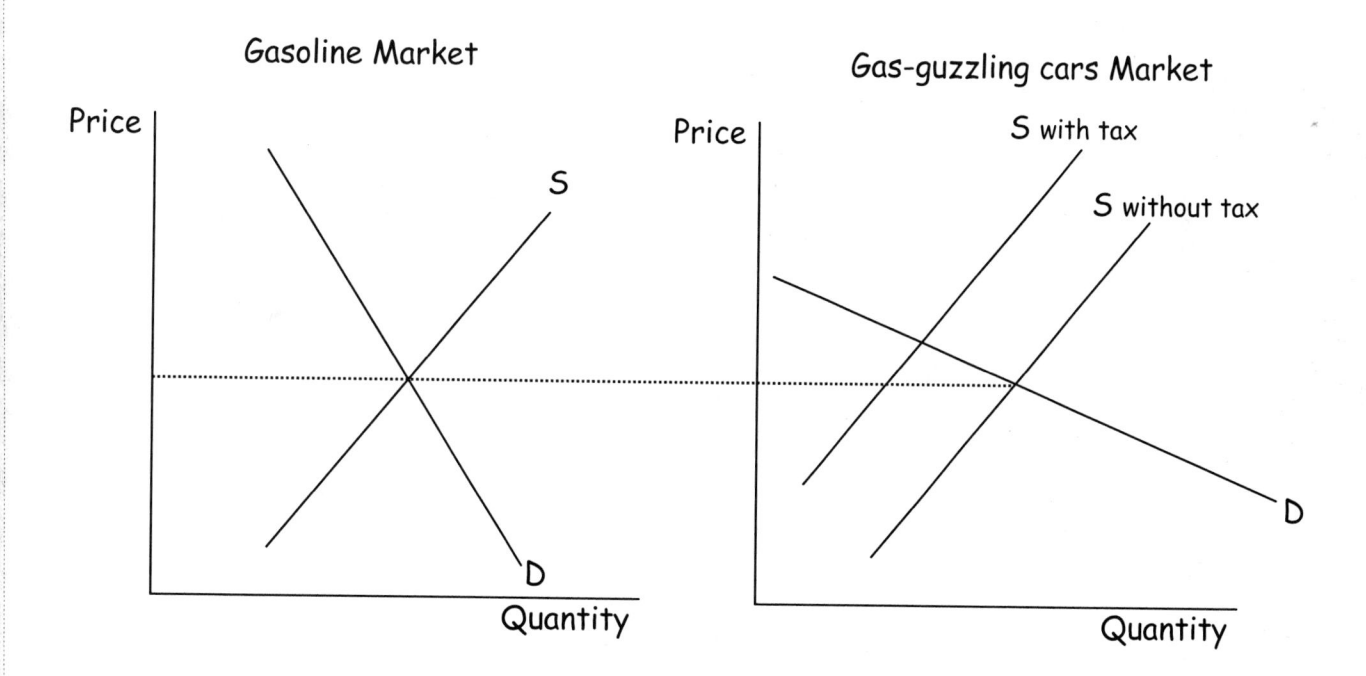

Gasoline Market

Price / Quantity
S, D

Gas-guzzling cars Market

Price / Quantity
S with tax, S without tax, D

ECON 102   Name:_____

Prof. Jose Vazquez-Cognet   TA:_____
                          More about Taxes

1. The state has decided to increase funding for public education. They are considering four
    alternative taxes to finance these expenditures. All four taxes would raise the same amount of
    revenue. These are the options the State is considering:
    i.   A sales tax on food.
    ii. A tax on families with school-age children.
    iii. A property tax on vacation homes.
    iv. A sales tax on jewelry.

    a. Taxes change incentives. How might individuals change their behavior because of
        each of these taxes?

    b. Rank these taxes from least deadweight loss to most deadweight loss. Explain.

    c. Is deadweight loss the only thing to consider when designing a tax system?

ECON 102   Name:_____

Prof. Jose Vazquez-Cognet   TA:_____
                     More about Taxes

1. The state has decided to increase funding for public education. They are considering four alternative taxes to finance these expenditures. All four taxes would raise the same amount of revenue. These are the options the State is considering:
    i. A sales tax on food.
    ii. A tax on families with school-age children.
    iii. A property tax on vacation homes.
    iv. A sales tax on jewelry.

    a. Taxes change incentives. How might individuals change their behavior because of each of these taxes?

    b. Rank these taxes from least deadweight loss to most deadweight loss. Explain.

    c. Is deadweight loss the only thing to consider when designing a tax system?

2. When Bill Clinton moved into the White House in 1993, he increased the federal income tax rates on high-income tax payers by about 40%. Nevertheless, more recently, our current President George W. Bush has adopted a completely different strategy. In his own words, the President's tax policy is one of: "lower income taxes for all...." (The President's Agenda for Tax Relief). Part of the President's tax relief plan will cut the top marginal tax rate, the tax on each additional dollar of income, from nearly 40 percent to 33 percent. But who's right and who's wrong? Many economists believe that the answer lies on the *elasticity of labor supply*. But....

   a. What do you think are the things that would determine how elastic is the supply for labor? Please list at least three.

   b. Do you think the supply for labor in the US is elastic or inelastic? Please explain.

   c. Based on your answers to (a) and (b) please use the diagram below to show the effect of an increase in the federal income tax rate on the US labor market. In your diagram, make sure to identify the following: (1) the loss in consumer; (2) the loss in producer surplus; (3) the loss in total surplus (the deadweight loss); (4) the revenue the government makes as a result of the tax.

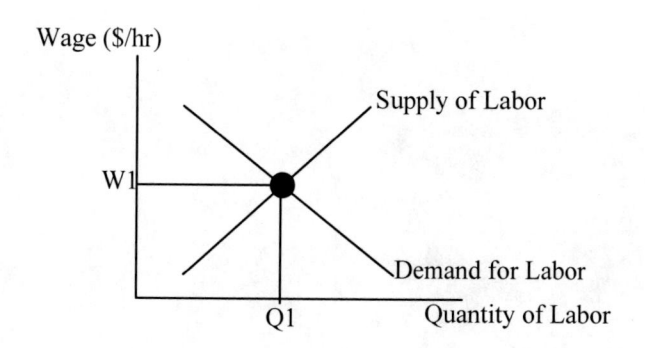

   d. Who do you think is right; Clinton or Bush? Please answer based on the impact of the tax on the quantity of labor (hint: this can be implied directly from the model you described in part c).

2. When Bill Clinton moved into the White House in 1993, he increased the federal income tax rates on high-income tax payers by about 40%. Nevertheless, more recently, our current President George W. Bush has adopted a completely different strategy. In his own words, the President's tax policy is one of: "lower income taxes for all...." (The President's Agenda for Tax Relief). Part of the President's tax relief plan will cut the top marginal tax rate, the tax on each additional dollar of income, from nearly 40 percent to 33 percent. But who's right and who's wrong? Many economists believe that the answer lies on the *elasticity of labor supply*. But....

   a. What do you think are the things that would determine how elastic is the supply for labor? Please list at least three.

   b. Do you think the supply for labor in the US is elastic or inelastic? Please explain.

   c. Based on your answers to (a) and (b) please use the diagram below to show the effect of an increase in the federal income tax rate on the US labor market. In your diagram, make sure to identify the following: (1) the loss in consumer; (2) the loss in producer surplus; (3) the loss in total surplus (the deadweight loss); (4) the revenue the government makes as a result of the tax.

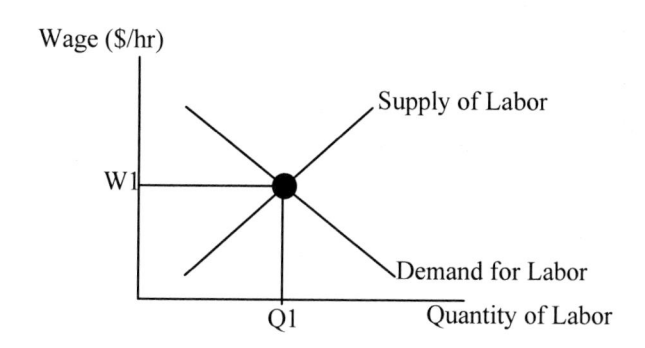

   d. Who do you think is right; Clinton or Bush? Please answer based on the impact of the tax on the quantity of labor (hint: this can be implied directly from the model you described in part c).

ECON 102   Name:_____

Prof. Jose Vazquez-Cognet   TA: _____

Managing Your Business Part I: Understanding the Costs of Staying in Business

For the next two weeks we will be discussing the *Theory of the Firm*. This economic theory describes the behavior of firms in competitive markets. In order to stimulate discussion, and to better understand the important concepts we will be discussing, I believe a good exercise is for students to imagine their own firm and then see how the concepts would apply to this business. Therefore, your assignment for today is to come up with your hypothetical business. Try to be imaginative; maybe someday you will have the change of starting up this business for real. In order to give you more structure, consider the following directions. I will illustrate each of the directions using my own dream business: a coffee shop around campus town (you are not allowed to compete against me on this market; too many of us already).

1. Coming up with your own firm/business.
    a. *Think small but do come up with name.* Try to be imaginative but within the realm of possibilities. Remember, you are just a recent graduate (or a school drop out) so finding enough capital might be a problem. The idea is that this will be a relatively small operation (Pizza parlor, a Car Wash, a Coffee House, a Computer Consulting firm, etc). Write up a brief description of your business including things such as 1) where is it going to be located; 2) which type of clientele would be serving; 3) what you consider will be your market niche, 4) anything else you may consider important to make the example more relevant in class.
        i. "The Wise Guy Coffee Shop" example: my coffee shop is relatively small; a few tables for two, a big round table for a big group and plenty of couches and big chairs I bought at a few garage sales and e-bay. It is located somewhere in the general area of the campus. I will serve a variety of coffees from different parts of the world. While I will provide the same coffee as other coffee houses around campus, I will try to differentiate my establishment by mainly two things: 1) connecting people to the coffee they are consuming, and 2) targeting the large group of what I called "social coffee drinkers". In other words, I will try offer a place for people to come and talk and discuss the news of day with other like-minded people. I want my coffee shop to be a "hang out" place for an interesting community of students and professors who, after some time, become invested with the location. The coffee house will provide an environment conducive to these goals.

2. *Defining your product.* Make sure you clearly define the product(s) your are going to study. Most firms will end up delivering more than one product. That's fine. But remember; simplify!. Therefore, I want you to identify only one of these products and for the purpose of the class concentrate on that one.
    a. "The Wise Coffee Shop" example: my business supplies a variety of food and beverages items (juices, sandwiches, desserts, etc). Nevertheless, I will concentrate mainly on the core of my business, which is coffee. Particularly, I will concentrate on cups of coffee serve; that will be my Output category.

ECON 102   Name:_____

Prof. Jose Vazquez-Cognet   TA: _____

Managing Your Business Part I: Understanding the Costs of Staying in Business

For the next two weeks we will be discussing the *Theory of the Firm*. This economic theory describes the behavior of firms in competitive markets. In order to stimulate discussion, and to better understand the important concepts we will be discussing, I believe a good exercise is for students to imagine their own firm and then see how the concepts would apply to this business. Therefore, your assignment for today is to come up with your hypothetical business. Try to be imaginative; maybe someday you will have the change of starting up this business for real. In order to give you more structure, consider the following directions. I will illustrate each of the directions using my own dream business: a coffee shop around campus town (you are not allowed to compete against me on this market; too many of us already).

1. Coming up with your own firm/business.
    a. *Think small but do come up with name.* Try to be imaginative but within the realm of possibilities. Remember, you are just a recent graduate (or a school drop out) so finding enough capital might be a problem. The idea is that this will be a relatively small operation (Pizza parlor, a Car Wash, a Coffee House, a Computer Consulting firm, etc). Write up a brief description of your business including things such as 1) where is it going to be located; 2) which type of clientele would be serving; 3) what you consider will be your market niche, 4) anything else you may consider important to make the example more relevant in class.
        i. "The Wise Guy Coffee Shop" example: my coffee shop is relatively small; a few tables for two, a big round table for a big group and plenty of couches and big chairs I bought at a few garage sales and e-bay. It is located somewhere in the general area of the campus. I will serve a variety of coffees from different parts of the world. While I will provide the same coffee as other coffee houses around campus, I will try to differentiate my establishment by mainly two things: 1) connecting people to the coffee they are consuming, and 2) targeting the large group of what I called "social coffee drinkers". In other words, I will try offer a place for people to come and talk and discuss the news of day with other like-minded people. I want my coffee shop to be a "hang out" place for an interesting community of students and professors who, after some time, become invested with the location. The coffee house will provide an environment conducive to these goals.

2. *Defining your product.* Make sure you clearly define the product(s) your are going to study. Most firms will end up delivering more than one product. That's fine. But remember; simplify!. Therefore, I want you to identify only one of these products and for the purpose of the class concentrate on that one.
    a. "The Wise Coffee Shop" example: my business supplies a variety of food and beverages items (juices, sandwiches, desserts, etc). Nevertheless, I will concentrate mainly on the core of my business, which is coffee. Particularly, I will concentrate on cups of coffee serve; that will be my Output category.

3. *Estimating your production function*: in order to help you focus your example in preparation for using it in class, use the following a table as a hypothetical information related to your business. Simply write the product you selected in part (2) in the column for Total Output. In order to apply this hypothetical numbers to your own case, simply play around with the time period. For instance, for my coffee shop, my units are "cups of coffee", so the numbers in the table make sense if we are talking about cups of coffee per day. If you decide to sell books, then the numbers might work better on a "per week" basis.

Table 1: The Production function.

Number of Workers per _____	Total Output (units of _____) per _____	Marginal Product Labor (MPL)
0	0	
1	100	
2	300	
3	350	
4	375	
5	390	
6	395	
7	398	

   a. *Marginal Product of Labor (MPL)*. Use the output and labor information from the table to calculate how your labor productivity changes as you add more and more workers (economists call this the *Marginal Product of Labor*). The equation for MPL is the following:

(0.1)
$$MPL = \frac{\Delta Q}{\Delta L} = \frac{(Q_2 - Q_1)}{(L_2 - L_1)}$$

   Enter this information on column # 3 of Table 1

4. *The Production Function and the MPL*. Now, use the graph paper at the end of this lab to draw the production function for your business. This is nothing more than a diagram with the Labor (L) on the a-axis and Output (Q) on the vertical axis. Once you're done with the diagram, answer the following questions based on that curve and the MPL you just calculated on part (3).
   a. What is the shape of your PF?

3. *Estimating your production function*: in order to help you focus your example in preparation for using it in class, use the following a table as a hypothetical information related to your business. Simply write the product you selected in part (2) in the column for Total Output. In order to apply this hypothetical numbers to your own case, simply play around with the time period. For instance, for my coffee shop, my units are "cups of coffee", so the numbers in the table make sense if we are talking about cups of coffee per day. If you decide to sell books, then the numbers might work better on a "per week" basis.

Table 1: The Production function.

Number of Workers per _____	Total Output (units of _____) per _____	Marginal Product Labor (MPL)
0	0	
1	100	
2	300	
3	350	
4	375	
5	390	
6	395	
7	398	

   a. *Marginal Product of Labor (MPL)*. Use the output and labor information from the table to calculate how your labor productivity changes as you add more and more workers (economists call this the *Marginal Product of Labor*). The equation for MPL is the following:

(0.1)
$$MPL = \frac{\Delta Q}{\Delta L} = \frac{(Q_2 - Q_1)}{(L_2 - L_1)}$$

Enter this information on column # 3 of Table 1

4. *The Production Function and the MPL.* Now, use the graph paper at the end of this lab to draw the production function for your business. This is nothing more than a diagram with the Labor (L) on the a-axis and Output (Q) on the vertical axis. Once you're done with the diagram, answer the following questions based on that curve and the MPL you just calculated on part (3).
   a. What is the shape of your PF?

b. Does it make sense for your business to have such a PF (shape)? Why?

c. Do you see this property also on the column of MPL? What is the relationship between the curve (PF) and the MPL?

5. *An evaluation of your costs*: O.k. so lets do the costs now. First, make a list of all the potential costs you will have to incur as a result of your business. Use the table below to list the most important of these costs. Make sure to include all costs: economic and accounting costs. Also, make sure to separate these costs between Fixed and Variable Costs. Also, try to come up with rough numbers for at least ONE of your variable costs (try to use labor) and ONE of your fixed costs (choose the most expensive fixed cost). *Remember, your costs must be specified in the same time period as your output. In other words, if your output is per day, then your cost must be specified as "per day". So, for something like "rent", which is usually paid on a monthly basis, you would have to divide that payment by 30 (average days in a month).*
    a. "The Wise Coffee Shop" example: my fixed costs are probably rent for the location, machinery, electric power, tables and other furniture. My variable costs are the wage for my employees, coffee cups and other supplies, and cost of my products. An example of opportunity costs is the salary I would make working on my own if I didn't have to work on the coffee shop; this is roughly the salary I make right now. Probably the most relevant variable cost for my business will be labor, for which a price of $56 per employee per day seems reasonable. An example of fixed cost could be the "espresso" machine, which I could rent for $45 per day.

Table 2: Your Different Types of Costs

| Fixed Costs || Variable Costs ||
Activity	Cost per unit	Type	Cost per unit
Rent		Labor	

b. *The Cost of Production.* Now we're going to try to fill **Table -3-(at the end of the lab)**
    i. Fixed Costs: Remember that I asked to think of ONE of the Fixed Costs associated with your production? Enter these costs on column # 3 of Table 3. For the time being we will assume these are the only Fixed Costs associated with your production.

b. Does it make sense for your business to have such a PF (shape)? Why?

c. Do you see this property also on the column of MPL? What is the relationship between the curve (PF) and the MPL?

5. *An evaluation of your costs*: O.k. so lets do the costs now. First, make a list of all the potential costs you will have to incur as a result of your business. Use the table below to list the most important of these costs. Make sure to include all costs: economic and accounting costs. Also, make sure to separate these costs between Fixed and Variable Costs. Also, try to come up with rough numbers for at least ONE of your variable costs (try to use labor) and ONE of your fixed costs (choose the most expensive fixed cost). *Remember, your costs must be specified in the same time period as your output. In other words, if your output is per day, then your cost must be specified as "per day". So, for something like "rent", which is usually paid on a monthly basis, you would have to divide that payment by 30 (average days in a month).*
   a. "The Wise Coffee Shop" example: my fixed costs are probably rent for the location, machinery, electric power, tables and other furniture. My variable costs are the wage for my employees, coffee cups and other supplies, and cost of my products. An example of opportunity costs is the salary I would make working on my own if I didn't have to work on the coffee shop; this is roughly the salary I make right now. Probably the most relevant variable cost for my business will be labor, for which a price of $56 per employee per day seems reasonable. An example of fixed cost could be the "espresso" machine, which I could rent for $45 per day.

Table 2: Your Different Types of Costs

Fixed Costs		Variable Costs	
Activity	Cost per unit	Type	Cost per unit
Rent		Labor	

b. *The Cost of Production.* Now we're going to try to fill **Table -3-(at the end of the lab)**
   i. Fixed Costs: Remember that I asked to think of ONE of the Fixed Costs associated with your production? Enter these costs on column # 3 of Table 3. For the time being we will assume these are the only Fixed Costs associated with your production.

ii. Now, how much you will pay to your employees per _____? For the time being, we will assume these will be the only variable costs of your business. You should now be able to calculate the values for column #4 of Table 3. What is the equation on column # 4? Write it down here: _____

ii. Now, how much you will pay to your employees per _____? For the time being, we will assume these will be the only variable costs of your business. You should now be able to calculate the values for column #4 of Table 3. What is the equation on column # 4? Write it down here:

_____

    iii. Calculate your total costs on column # 5 (TC = VC + FC).

6. *Per Unit Analysis.* Now, to better use your cost information, you will probably need to have it on a "per-unit" basis. Therefore, we need to know not only the **TOTAL COSTS**, but also the **AVEREAGE COSTS** of production. Use the following equations to calculate the Average Fixed Costs (AFC), the Average Variable Costs (AVC) and Average Total Costs (ATC) of your business. Enter these values on the corresponding columns of Table 3.

$$AFC = \frac{FC}{Q}$$

$$AVC = \frac{VC}{Q}$$

$$ATC = \frac{TC}{Q}$$

    i. Lets study these columns for a second. Imagine you had to draw the values of these columns in the following diagram: how would the shape of each curve would look like? (***Draw one curve for each column: the numbers are not important; just the shape***)

Costs

Quantity of _____

        a. What is the general shape of the AFC curve? Does this makes sense? Explain.

        b. What is the general shape of the AVC curve? Does this makes sense? Explain.

iii. Calculate your total costs on column # 5 (TC = VC + FC).

6. *Per Unit Analysis.* Now, to better use your cost information, you will probably need to have it on a "per-unit" basis. Therefore, we need to know not only the **TOTAL COSTS**, but also the **AVEREAGE COSTS** of production. Use the following equations to calculate the Average Fixed Costs (AFC), the Average Variable Costs (AVC) and Average Total Costs (ATC) of your business. Enter these values on the corresponding columns of Table 3.

$$AFC = \frac{FC}{Q}$$

$$AVC = \frac{VC}{Q}$$

$$ATC = \frac{TC}{Q}$$

    i. Lets study these columns for a second. Imagine you had to draw the values of these columns in the following diagram: how would the shape of each curve would look like? (***Draw one curve for each column: the numbers are not important; just the shape***)

Costs

Quantity of _____

        a. What is the general shape of the AFC curve? Does this makes sense? Explain.

        b. What is the general shape of the AVC curve? Does this makes sense? Explain.

c. What is the general shape of the ATC curve? Does this makes sense? Explain.

d. Can you identify any relationship between the different curves in the chart so far? Explain.

7. Now, we have one more cost measure and we're done with the costs. In order to understand how efficient your business is you will need to know not only how much are your costs per unit of output (average) but also how much your Total Costs change as you increase your output by an additional unit (marginal unit). These costs are called your Marginal Costs of production. The formal equation for MC is the following:

$$MC = \frac{\Delta TC}{\Delta Q} = \frac{(TC_2 - TC_1)}{(Q_2 - Q_1)}$$

Use this formula to calculate the MC of your production and enter them in column # 9 of your table. Also, once you're done add this curve to your diagram above.

ii. What is the shape of the curve? Does it make sense?

iii. Can you identify any relationship between the MC curve and the other curves on the diagram?

c. What is the general shape of the ATC curve? Does this makes sense? Explain.

d. Can you identify any relationship between the different curves in the chart so far? Explain.

7. Now, we have one more cost measure and we're done with the costs. In order to understand how efficient your business is you will need to know not only how much are your costs per unit of output (average) but also how much your Total Costs change as you increase your output by an additional unit (marginal unit). These costs are called your Marginal Costs of production. The formal equation for MC is the following:

$$MC = \frac{\Delta TC}{\Delta Q} = \frac{(TC_2 - TC_1)}{(Q_2 - Q_1)}$$

Use this formula to calculate the MC of your production and enter them in column # 9 of your table. Also, once you're done add this curve to your diagram above.

ii. What is the shape of the curve? Does it make sense?

iii. Can you identify any relationship between the MC curve and the other curves on the diagram?

Table # 2: Costs, Revenues, and Profit for Your Dream Business.

Labor (1)	Output (2)	Fixed Cost (3)	Variable Cost (4)	Total Cost (5)	Average Fixed Cost (6)	Average Variable Cost (7)	Average Total Cost (8)	Marginal Cost (9)	Price (10)	Total Revenue (11)	Profit (12)	Marginal Revenue (13)
0	0				---	---	---					
1	100											
2	300											
3	350											
4	375											
5	390											
6	395											
7	398											

Table # 2: Costs, Revenues, and Profit for Your Dream Business.

Labor (1)	Output (2)	Fixed Cost (3)	Variable Cost (4)	Total Cost (5)	Average Fixed Cost (6)	Average Variable Cost (7)	Average Total Cost (8)	Marginal Cost (9)	Price (10)	Total Revenue (11)	Profit (12)	Marginal Revenue (13)
0	0				---	---	---					
1	100											
2	300											
3	350											
4	375											
5	390											
6	395											
7	398											

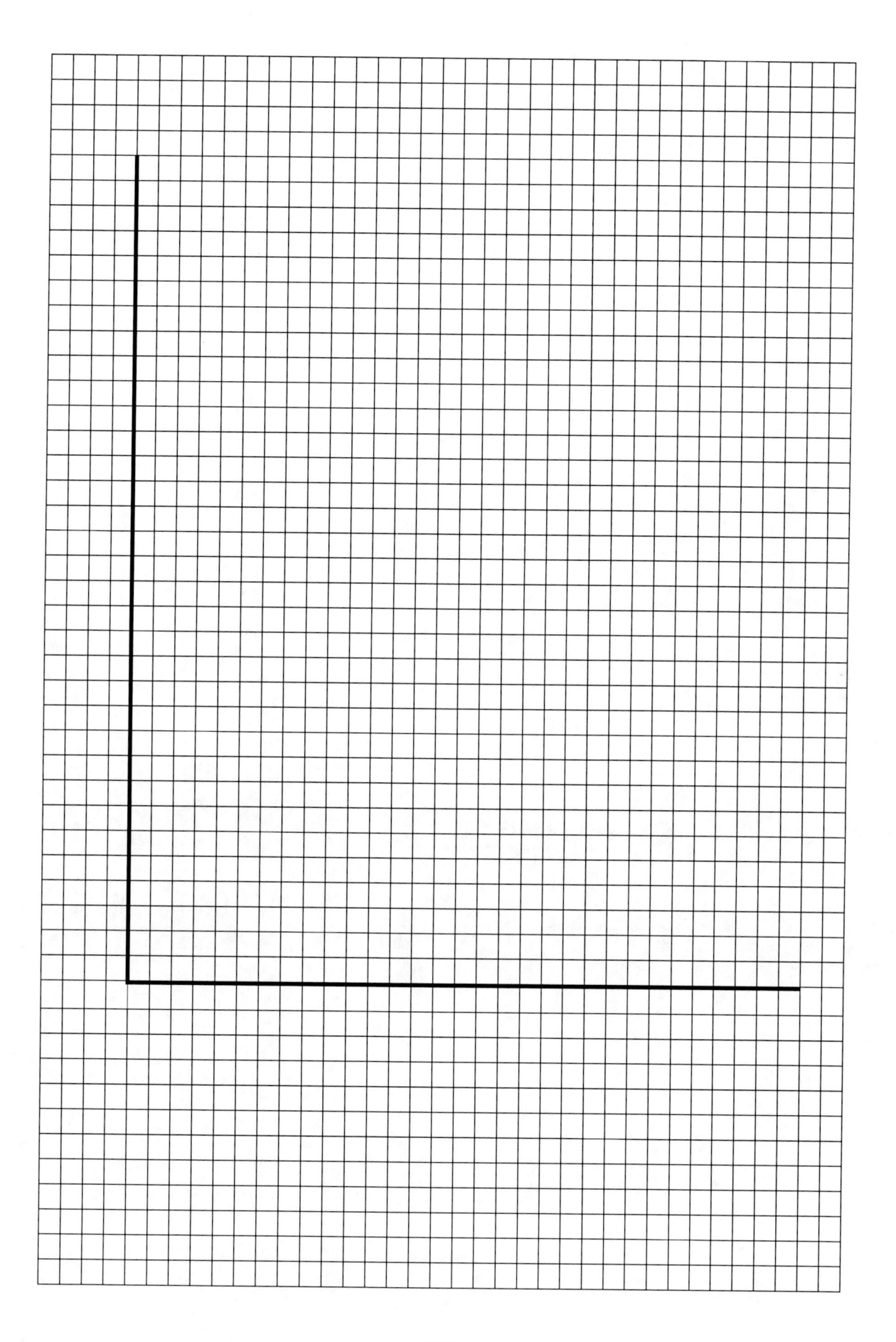

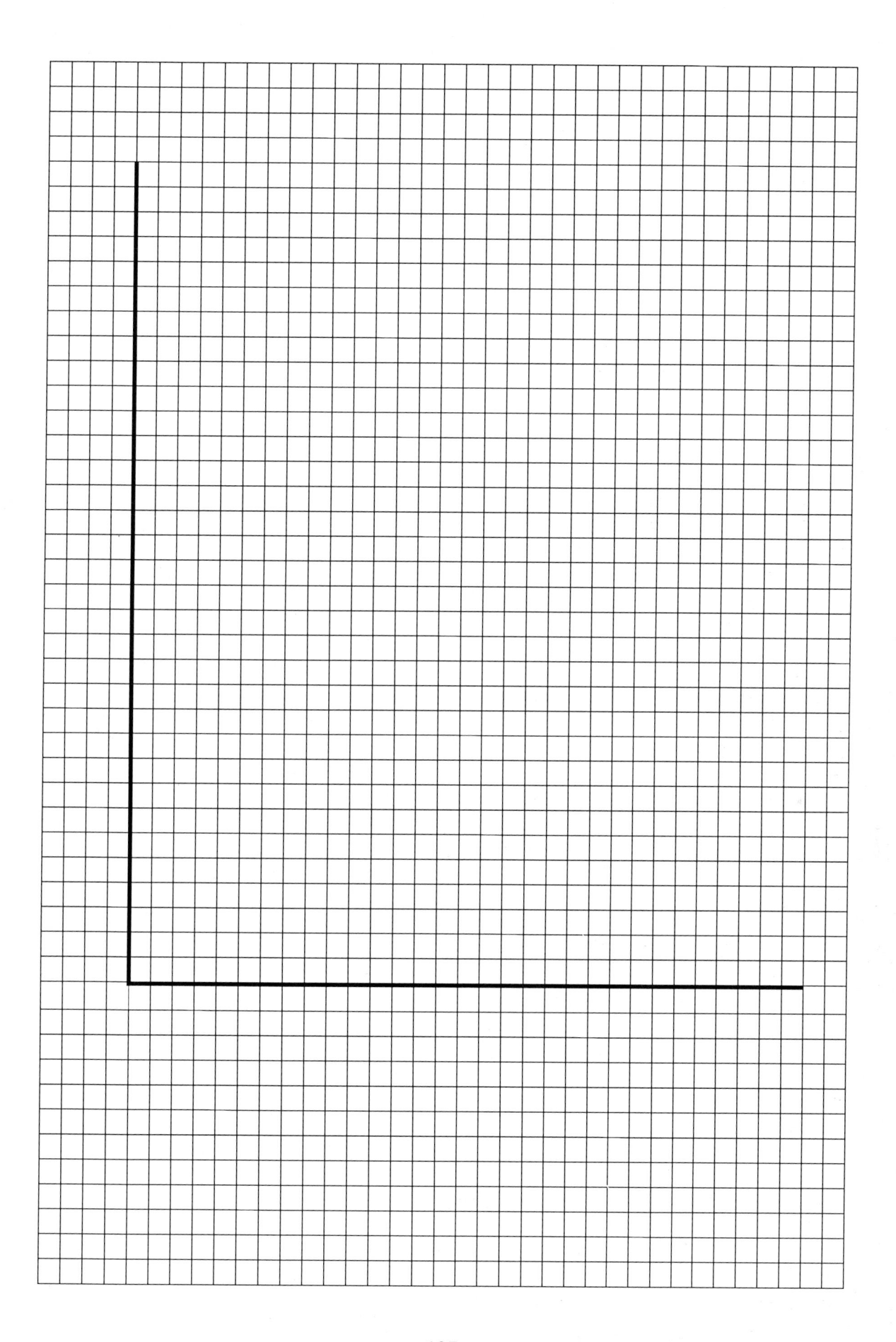

ECON 102   Name:_____

Prof. Jose Vazquez-Cognet   TA:_____

Managing Your Business Part II: Choosing How Much to Produce

Now that we understand the cost of doing business, it's time to make the most important decision as a business owner/manager: *decide how much to produce?*

In order to simplify things a little for you; let's continue to use the numbers from my dream business; The Wise Guy Coffee Shop. As you go along, feel free to apply what we do here to your own example; for now you're my business partner. Here are the number we had calculated last week for the Coffee House.

Table # 1: Revenues, Costs and Profits

Labor (1)	Output (2)	Total Cost (3)	Marginal Costs (4)	Average Fixed Cost (5)	Average Variable Cost (6)	Average Total Cost (7)	Price (8)	Total Revenue (9)	Marginal Revenue (10)	Profit (11)
0	0	$45		----	----	----				
			$0.56							
1	100	$101		$0.45	$0.56	$1.01				
			$0.28							
2	300	$157		$0.15	$0.37	$0.52				
			$1.12							
3	350	$213		$0.13	$0.48	$0.61				
			$2.24							
4	375	$269		$0.12	$0.60	$0.72				
			$3.73							
5	390	$325		$0.12	$0.72	$0.83				
			$11.20							
6	395	$381		$0.11	$0.85	$0.96				
			$18.67							
7	398	$437		$0.11	$0.98	$1.10				

As you can see, there are four columns left to be calculated, so that's what we're going to do today.

1. Column # 8: The first thing we need to do is to come up with a price to charge for our cups of coffee. Enter this information in the table above (column #8). Aha, now you're wondering: should I enter the same price for each category of output?
    a. What do you think, would we be able to change the price of the cups of coffee we sell depending on how many of them we sell?

ECON 102   Name:_____

Prof. Jose Vazquez-Cognet   TA:_____

Managing Your Business Part II: Choosing How Much to Produce

Now that we understand the cost of doing business, it's time to make the most important decision as a business owner/manager: *decide how much to produce?*

In order to simplify things a little for you; let's continue to use the numbers from my dream business; The Wise Guy Coffee Shop. As you go along, feel free to apply what we do here to your own example; for now you're my business partner. Here are the number we had calculated last week for the Coffee House.

Table # 1: Revenues, Costs and Profits

Labor (1)	Output (2)	Total Cost (3)	Marginal Costs (4)	Average Fixed Cost (5)	Average Variable Cost (6)	Average Total Cost (7)	Price (8)	Total Revenue (9)	Marginal Revenue (10)	Profit (11)
0	0	$45		----	----	----				
			$0.56							
1	100	$101		$0.45	$0.56	$1.01				
			$0.28							
2	300	$157		$0.15	$0.37	$0.52				
			$1.12							
3	350	$213		$0.13	$0.48	$0.61				
			$2.24							
4	375	$269		$0.12	$0.60	$0.72				
			$3.73							
5	390	$325		$0.12	$0.72	$0.83				
			$11.20							
6	395	$381		$0.11	$0.85	$0.96				
			$18.67							
7	398	$437		$0.11	$0.98	$1.10				

As you can see, there are four columns left to be calculated, so that's what we're going to do today.

1. Column # 8: The first thing we need to do is to come up with a price to charge for our cups of coffee. Enter this information in the table above (column #8). Aha, now you're wondering: should I enter the same price for each category of output?
    a. What do you think, would we be able to change the price of the cups of coffee we sell depending on how many of them we sell?

2. Now that we know the price, we have all the information we need to calculate the rest of the columns.
    a. Column # 9: To calculate the Total Revenue (TR) of your business simply multiply the amount of coffee cups we sell by the price of each cup of coffee (TR = P * Q).

    b. Column # 10: As was the case with the costs, it will be useful to know how much your revenue change as you change your production by 1 unit: this is call your **Marginal Revenue (MR)**. The formula for it is:

    $$MR = \frac{\Delta TR}{\Delta Q} = \frac{(TR_2 - TR_1)}{(Q_2 - Q_1)}$$

    Use this formula to calculate column #10. Do you notice anything interesting? Can you explain this?

    c. Column # 11: So we are ready to calculate the most important piece of information: you Profits (π). The profits are nothing more than the value of your output after you pay for producing it. Formally,

    $$\text{Profits} = \pi = TR - TC$$

    Use this formula to calculate the values for column # 11.

3. So, how many units of coffee we should sell in order to maximize our profits?

    a. Do you notice something interesting at the point that we maximize our profits?

    b. Can you give an economic reasoning (in words) as to the relationship between MR and MC at the profit maximizing level of output?

2. Now that we know the price, we have all the information we need to calculate the rest of the columns.
   a. Column # 9: To calculate the Total Revenue (TR) of your business simply multiply the amount of coffee cups we sell by the price of each cup of coffee (TR = P * Q).

   b. Column # 10: As was the case with the costs, it will be useful to know how much your revenue change as you change your production by 1 unit: this is call your **Marginal Revenue (MR)**. The formula for it is:

   $$MR = \frac{\Delta TR}{\Delta Q} = \frac{(TR_2 - TR_1)}{(Q_2 - Q_1)}$$

   Use this formula to calculate column #10. Do you notice anything interesting? Can you explain this?

   c. Column # 11: So we are ready to calculate the most important piece of information: you Profits (π). The profits are nothing more than the value of your output after you pay for producing it. Formally,

   $$\text{Profits} = \pi = TR - TC$$

   Use this formula to calculate the values for column # 11.

3. So, how many units of coffee we should sell in order to maximize our profits?

   a. Do you notice something interesting at the point that we maximize our profits?

   b. Can you give an economic reasoning (in words) as to the relationship between MR and MC at the profit maximizing level of output?

ECON 102

Name:_____

Prof. Jose Vazquez-Cognet

TA: _____

MONOPOLY

Understanding Market Structures

1. Given the description of the different categories of market structures we just explained, please classify the following firms as either Perfect Competition, Monopoly, Monopolistic Competition or Oligopoly. In each case, also explain what is the source of their market power (if they do in fact have market power)? Explain.

    a. Anheuser-Busch?

    b. Microsoft's Windows OS?

    c. Regional Electric Utilities?

    d. College Bookstore?

    e. Starbucks?

    f. The Chicago Cubs?

    g. Greyhound Bus?

    h. United Airlines?

2. Which of the business above would be able to use price discrimination as a way to increase profits? Can you give an example of each case?

ECON 102   Name:_____

Prof. Jose Vazquez-Cognet   TA: _____

MONOPOLY

Understanding Market Structures

1. Given the description of the different categories of market structures we just explained, please classify the following firms as either Perfect Competition, Monopoly, Monopolistic Competition or Oligopoly. In each case, also explain what is the source of their market power (if they do in fact have market power)? Explain.

    a. Anheuser-Busch?

    b. Microsoft's Windows OS?

    c. Regional Electric Utilities?

    d. College Bookstore?

    e. Starbucks?

    f. The Chicago Cubs?

    g. Greyhound Bus?

    h. United Airlines?

2. Which of the business above would be able to use price discrimination as a way to increase profits? Can you give an example of each case?

Review Questions and Applications of the Theory of the Firm

3. If the marginal cost of production is increasing, does this tell you whether the average variable cost is increasing or decreasing? Explain.

4. The combination of the DVD player, the flat plasma screen, and the surround sound has revolutionized watching a movie at home. At the same time, advances in technology in the movie theater have raised the standard that the home entertainment alternative must achieve. Think about the effects of these technological changes on competitive markets for goods and services that are influenced by movie going and home movie watching. You must identify at least two different markets that would be affected by these technologies. On each case, your job is to do the following
    a. Identify the market(s) for one related good or service that will expand and one that will contract as a result of the change in technology.
    b. Using diagrams, identify the initial equilibrium at both the industry and firm level on both markets.
    c. Describe in detail (and with diagrams) the sequence of events as the two markets you've identified respond to the new technologies.
    d. Identify the final equilibrium at both the industry and firm level on both markets.

5. At the beginning of the twentieth century, there were many small American automobile manufacturers. At the end of the century, there are only three large ones. Suppose that this situation is not the result of lax federal enforcement of antimonopoly laws. How do you explain the decrease in the number of manufacturers? (*Hint: What is the inherent cost structure of the automobile industry?*)

6. In 1968 the airline industry approach was the following: Total Cost of the airline for the year was divided by the number of flights during the year (TC/Q). This came to about $4,000 for the typical flight. Since a jet had to be 65% full in order to earn the ticket sales of $4,000 the main rule was: offer a flight if, and only if, on average, 65% of the seats could be filled with paying passengers, since only then could the flight break even. Yet Continental challenged this. Not only it was flying jets filled to just 50% capacity, but it was actually expanding flight on many routes. And surprising everyone, its profits went up (higher than all other airlines). How come? Please explain.

7. Before 1991, the eight Ivy league colleges (Brown, Columbia, Cornell, Dartmouth, Harvard, Princeton, Penn, and Yale), along with MIT, shared information and agreed on rules for setting their prices of education (price equals tuition minus scholarship). Since 1991, these schools have set their prices in competition with each other. Using a diagram, compare the market fro an Ivy League education before and after 1991. Predict what has happened to the efficiency of the market, to the distribution of producer and consumer surplus, and to deadweight loss.

8. Assume a computer firm's marginal costs of production are constant at $1,000 per computer. However, the fixed costs of production are equal to $10,000.
    a. Calculate the firm's average variable cost and average total cost curves.
    b. If the firm wanted to minimize the average total cost of production, would it choose to be very large or very small? Explain.

Review Questions and Applications of the Theory of the Firm

3. If the marginal cost of production is increasing, does this tell you whether the average variable cost is increasing or decreasing? Explain.

4. The combination of the DVD player, the flat plasma screen, and the surround sound has revolutionized watching a movie at home. At the same time, advances in technology in the movie theater have raised the standard that the home entertainment alternative must achieve. Think about the effects of these technological changes on competitive markets for goods and services that are influenced by movie going and home movie watching. You must identify at least two different markets that would be affected by these technologies. On each case, your job is to do the following
    a. Identify the market(s) for one related good or service that will expand and one that will contract as a result of the change in technology.
    b. Using diagrams, identify the initial equilibrium at both the industry and firm level on both markets.
    c. Describe in detail (and with diagrams) the sequence of events as the two markets you've identified respond to the new technologies.
    d. Identify the final equilibrium at both the industry and firm level on both markets.

5. At the beginning of the twentieth century, there were many small American automobile manufacturers. At the end of the century, there are only three large ones. Suppose that this situation is not the result of lax federal enforcement of antimonopoly laws. How do you explain the decrease in the number of manufacturers? (*Hint: What is the inherent cost structure of the automobile industry?*)

6. In 1968 the airline industry approach was the following: Total Cost of the airline for the year was divided by the number of flights during the year (TC/Q). This came to about $4,000 for the typical flight. Since a jet had to be 65% full in order to earn the ticket sales of $4,000 the main rule was: offer a flight if, and only if, on average, 65% of the seats could be filled with paying passengers, since only then could the flight break even. Yet Continental challenged this. Not only it was flying jets filled to just 50% capacity, but it was actually expanding flight on many routes. And surprising everyone, its profits went up (higher than all other airlines). How come? Please explain.

7. Before 1991, the eight Ivy league colleges (Brown, Columbia, Cornell, Dartmouth, Harvard, Princeton, Penn, and Yale), along with MIT, shared information and agreed on rules for setting their prices of education (price equals tuition minus scholarship). Since 1991, these schools have set their prices in competition with each other. Using a diagram, compare the market fro an Ivy League education before and after 1991. Predict what has happened to the efficiency of the market, to the distribution of producer and consumer surplus, and to deadweight loss.

8. Assume a computer firm's marginal costs of production are constant at $1,000 per computer. However, the fixed costs of production are equal to $10,000.
    a. Calculate the firm's average variable cost and average total cost curves.
    b. If the firm wanted to minimize the average total cost of production, would it choose to be very large or very small? Explain.

9. Why is there a social cost to monopoly power? If the gains to producers from monopoly power could be redistributed to consumers, would the social cost of monopoly power be eliminated? Explain briefly.

9. Why is there a social cost to monopoly power? If the gains to producers from monopoly power could be redistributed to consumers, would the social cost of monopoly power be eliminated? Explain briefly.

ECON 102   Name:_____

Prof. Jose Vazquez - Cognet   TA: _____

Externalities: the Economics of Pollution

Film Clip Analysis: Erin Brockovich

Julia Roberts won Best Actress for her portrayal of Erin Brockovich. The film is based on the true story of Brockovich, a single mother with no formal education, few prospects for employment, and down on her luck. Eventually, she gets a job as a file clerk for small law firm. There she begins to investigate (on her own) illnesses in a small town caused by the illegal dumping of deadly toxic waste by Pacific Gas & Electric. Spurred on by her efforts at uncovering the truth, the law firm she works for becomes involved in one of the largest class action lawsuits in history, resulting in a settlement of over $300 million!

We are going to watch two short scenes from the movie. In the first scene Ed Masry (Albert Finney) and Erin Brockovich meet with a representative of Pacific Gas & Electric (PG&E) to discuss a settlement offer from the firm. The company offers compensates the claimants for the value of the land they own, but no compensation is offered for medical damages as a result of toxic poisoning.

On the second scene, later during the movie, the company has sent two more layers to negotiate but the offer is still below what Erin and Masry thinks it should be.

After watching the clip, we will discuss the following questions. In preparation, take some time and write a short answer to each of these questions. Feel free to discuss each of them with the students next to you (in fact, I encourage you to do this).

1. PG&E decided to dump toxic poison, rather than clean it up. Describe how this decision lowered the firm's *private costs* but raised the *social cost* to society.

_____

_____

_____

_____

_____

ECON 102   Name:_____

Prof. Jose Vazquez - Cognet   TA: _____

Externalities: the Economics of Pollution

Film Clip Analysis: Erin Brockovich

Julia Roberts won Best Actress for her portrayal of Erin Brockovich. The film is based on the true story of Brockovich, a single mother with no formal education, few prospects for employment, and down on her luck. Eventually, she gets a job as a file clerk for small law firm. There she begins to investigate (on her own) illnesses in a small town caused by the illegal dumping of deadly toxic waste by Pacific Gas & Electric. Spurred on by her efforts at uncovering the truth, the law firm she works for becomes involved in one of the largest class action lawsuits in history, resulting in a settlement of over $300 million!

We are going to watch two short scenes from the movie. In the first scene Ed Masry (Albert Finney) and Erin Brockovich meet with a representative of Pacific Gas & Electric (PG&E) to discuss a settlement offer from the firm. The company offers compensates the claimants for the value of the land they own, but no compensation is offered for medical damages as a result of toxic poisoning.

On the second scene, later during the movie, the company has sent two more layers to negotiate but the offer is still below what Erin and Masry thinks it should be.

After watching the clip, we will discuss the following questions. In preparation, take some time and write a short answer to each of these questions. Feel free to discuss each of them with the students next to you (in fact, I encourage you to do this).

1. PG&E decided to dump toxic poison, rather than clean it up. Describe how this decision lowered the firm's *private costs* but raised the *social cost* to society.

   _____

   _____

   _____

   _____

   _____

2. What do you think will happen to the price of electricity offered by PG&E if the government imposed a Bann on the production of toxic poisons?

3. Who would be better off if society banned the production of toxic poisons?

4. What would be another way of solving the problem (i.e. reducing pollution by PG&E) as an alternative to banning the production of toxic poisons?

2. What do you think will happen to the price of electricity offered by PG&E if the government imposed a Bann on the production of toxic poisons?

3. Who would be better off if society banned the production of toxic poisons?

4. What would be another way of solving the problem (i.e. reducing pollution by PG&E) as an alternative to banning the production of toxic poisons?

ECON 102

Prof. Jose Vazquez

Name:_____

TA: _____

Externalities: the Private Solution (Coase Theorem)

I never really told you if the guy speaking on the cell phone next to me at the coffee took my offer, right? Well, before I do that, let's evaluate my decision to offer him the $10. Was I being stupid by proposing this agreement? In order to do this, lets use the table below, which describes the social costs and benefits of the situation.

Obviously, these are hypothetical numbers. On the one hand, they assume I am able to put a value (in dollar terms) to how much suffering I get from listening to this guy on the cell phone. So for instance, when he makes his first call, my suffering is equal to $2.00 *(Social Costs)*. On the other hand, this scenario also assumes the guy next to me is able to put a value on the benefits he receives from making each call. So for instance, the value of the first call to him is $12 *(Private Benefits)*..

Table 1: Costs and Benefits of the Externality.

# of cell phone calls made	Total Social Costs per Call	Marginal Social Costs (MSC)	Total Private Benefits per call	Marginal Private Benefits (MPB)
0	$0		$0	
		$2		$12
1	$2		$12	
		$4		$10
2	$6		$22	
		$6		$8
3	$12		$30	
		$8		$6
4	$20		$36	
		$10		$4
5	$30		$40	

1. So, let see if you understand the intuition behind this table. How much is the value I have for Total Complete Silence (zero cell phone calls by strangers sitting around me) in the Coffee Shop on Sunday morning?

2. O.k. now, suppose the guy was thinking of making 5 cell phone calls that day. Given the numbers in the table, do you think I would be able to bribe him into not making at least 1 of the 5 calls? Why or why not?

ECON 102   Name:_____

Prof. Jose Vazquez   TA: _____

Externalities: the Private Solution (Coase Theorem)

I never really told you if the guy speaking on the cell phone next to me at the coffee took my offer, right? Well, before I do that, let's evaluate my decision to offer him the $10. Was I being stupid by proposing this agreement? In order to do this, lets use the table below, which describes the social costs and benefits of the situation.

Obviously, these are hypothetical numbers. On the one hand, they assume I am able to put a value (in dollar terms) to how much suffering I get from listening to this guy on the cell phone. So for instance, when he makes his first call, my suffering is equal to $2.00 *(Social Costs)*. On the other hand, this scenario also assumes the guy next to me is able to put a value on the benefits he receives from making each call. So for instance, the value of the first call to him is $12 *(Private Benefits)*..

Table 1: Costs and Benefits of the Externality.

# of cell phone calls made	Total Social Costs per Call	Marginal Social Costs (MSC)	Total Private Benefits per call	Marginal Private Benefits (MPB)
0	$0		$0	
		$2		$12
1	$2		$12	
		$4		$10
2	$6		$22	
		$6		$8
3	$12		$30	
		$8		$6
4	$20		$36	
		$10		$4
5	$30		$40	

1. So, let see if you understand the intuition behind this table. How much is the value I have for Total Complete Silence (zero cell phone calls by strangers sitting around me) in the Coffee Shop on Sunday morning?

2. O.k. now, suppose the guy was thinking of making 5 cell phone calls that day. Given the numbers in the table, do you think I would be able to bribe him into not making at least 1 of the 5 calls? Why or why not?

3. How many phone calls would I be able to prevent him from making if I simply pay him for his silence? Explain.

4. Now suppose I have the rights to a cell phone free environment. This means that the coffee shop has the following policy posted on a sign: *If you want to use your cell phone you need to get permission from the other customers first.* Given this policy, do you think he (the annoying cell phone guy) would be able to bribe me into making his first phone call? How many phone calls he will end up making?

5. What did we learn?

3. How many phone calls would I be able to prevent him from making if I simply pay him for his silence? Explain.

4. Now suppose I have the rights to a cell phone free environment. This means that the coffee shop has the following policy posted on a sign: *If you want to use your cell phone you need to get permission from the other customers first.* Given this policy, do you think he (the annoying cell phone guy) would be able to bribe me into making his first phone call? How many phone calls he will end up making?

5. What did we learn?

ECON 102   Name:_____

Prof. Jose Vazquez-Cognet   TA: _____
LAB # 20

The Tragedy of the Commons

Suppose that fish cost a dollar a pound, and the marginal cost of running a vessel – including the fuel and salaries for crew and owner – is $250 per day. Further, assume the relation between the number of vessels and the total catch is given by the following table and figure:

# of Vessels	Total Catch (lbs)
1	400
2	800
3	1200
4	1600
5	1900
6	2100
7	2100
8	2000

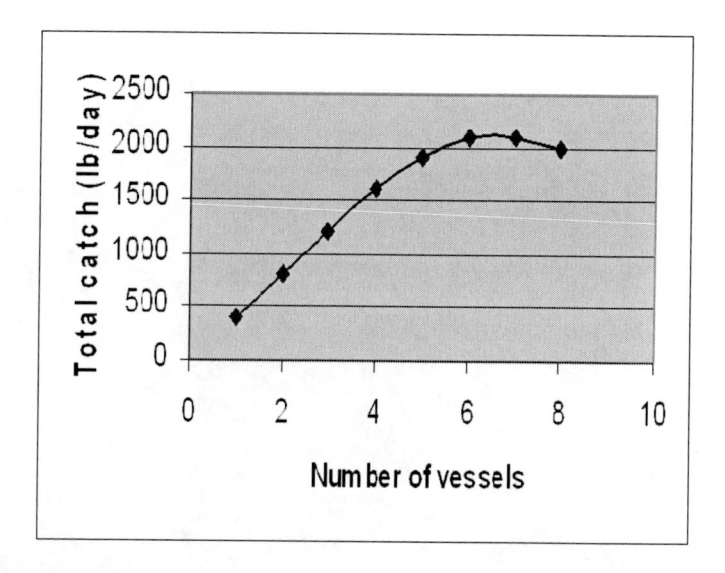

1. If there was open access to the bay and seven boats were already fishing, would you fish in the bay?

2. If you ran the government fisheries board, how many boats would you allow out if you wanted to maximize total profits from the bay?

ECON 102   Name:_____

Prof. Jose Vazquez-Cognet   TA: _____
LAB # 20

The Tragedy of the Commons

Suppose that fish cost a dollar a pound, and the marginal cost of running a vessel – including the fuel and salaries for crew and owner – is $250 per day. Further, assume the relation between the number of vessels and the total catch is given by the following table and figure:

# of Vessels	Total Catch (lbs)
1	400
2	800
3	1200
4	1600
5	1900
6	2100
7	2100
8	2000

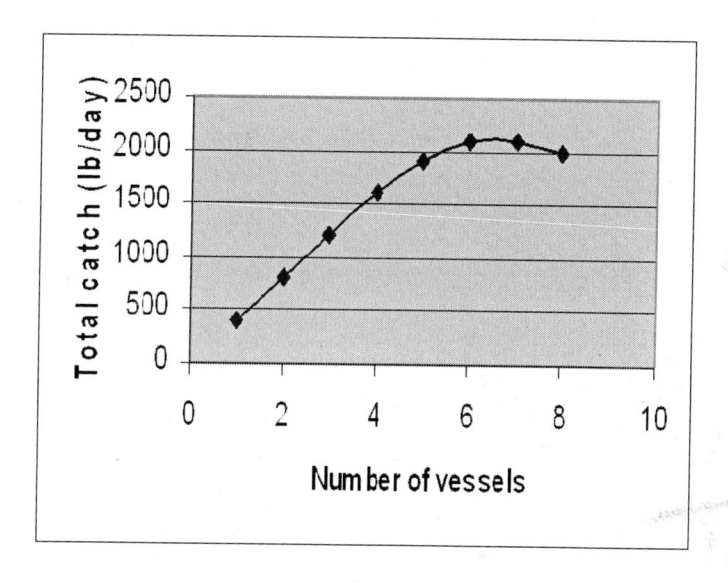

1. If there was open access to the bay and seven boats were already fishing, would you fish in the bay?

2. If you ran the government fisheries board, how many boats would you allow out if you wanted to maximize total profits from the bay?

147

ECON 102   Name:_____

Prof. Jose Vazquez-Cognet   TA: _____

Public Goods and Common Resources

The topic of Public Goods and Common Resources (Chapter 20) is truly one of the most interesting in any Intro to Micro course such as this one. After understanding these topics you will be able to understand the basic problems behind such social maladies as traffic congestion and resource over-consumption. But before we talk about the problem, we need to understand what is it that we are talking about here.

1. In each of the following cases, please answer the following two questions:

    o Is this situation an example of a private good, a public good or a common resource? Please classify each of the goods represented in this situation base on the classifications of goods we just presented (i.e. excludability and rivalry)
    o Is the problem of "free-riding" present in this situation? Please explain how.

    a. Buying a nice shirt at The Gap.

    b. Congested highways in the city of Chicago.

    c. National Defense in the United States

    d. Asking questions during class or during review sessions in this course.

    e. Going to vote during elections in this country.

    f. Public Education in the United States.

    g. Visiting Yellowstone National Park

    h. Downloading MP3 songs from the Web.

ECON 102   Name:_____

Prof. Jose Vazquez-Cognet   TA: _____

Public Goods and Common Resources

The topic of Public Goods and Common Resources (Chapter 20) is truly one of the most interesting in any Intro to Micro course such as this one. After understanding these topics you will be able to understand the basic problems behind such social maladies as traffic congestion and resource over-consumption. But before we talk about the problem, we need to understand what is it that we are talking about here.

1. In each of the following cases, please answer the following two questions:

    - Is this situation an example of a private good, a public good or a common resource? Please classify each of the goods represented in this situation base on the classifications of goods we just presented (i.e. excludability and rivalry)
    - Is the problem of "free-riding" present in this situation? Please explain how.

    a. Buying a nice shirt at The Gap.

    b. Congested highways in the city of Chicago.

    c. National Defense in the United States

    d. Asking questions during class or during review sessions in this course.

    e. Going to vote during elections in this country.

    f. Public Education in the United States.

    g. Visiting Yellowstone National Park

    h. Downloading MP3 songs from the Web.